How to Use Outsourcing to Grow Your Small Business

SCALE!: *How to Make Six Figures or More and Free Up Your Time to Live Life on Your Terms*

**By
Franklyn White**

TABLE OF CONTENTS

Introduction

Growing a small business through outsourcing is a concept and practice I am very familiar with. As a small business owner, I initially struggled to grow one of my first small businesses (a book/audiobook publishing business). But when I finally began deploying the outsourcing tips, techniques, and strategies I will share with you in this book, my business exploded and even allowed me to go into other areas of business, such as publishing mobile apps. But of just as much importance (if not of greater importance), when I started using outsourcing in my business, it freed up more of my time so that I could spend more time with my family, devote more time to my hobbies, travel, and live life on my own terms instead of being a slave to my business.

Today, we have over 30 people from around the world who work remotely for us doing numerous different tasks ranging from writing books, creating social media content, narrating audiobooks, providing graphic design, providing customer support, developing mobile apps, and much more. We've grown from a business that once only published books and audiobooks to a publishing business that is now just as active in the mobile app publishing arena. Contrary to popular belief, you do not have to have a huge budget to get started with outsourcing. You can get started on a very tight budget. I recommend starting slow by hiring just one employee at a time.

Chapter 1: The Importance of Developing an Outsourcing Mindset

I will return to this theme more than once in this book. That's because having or developing an outsourcing mindset is the most important factor for becoming successful at outsourcing.

In the journey of growing a small or home-based business, the transition from a do-it-all-yourself mindset to an outsourcing mindset is pivotal. Many entrepreneurs fall into the trap of believing they must handle every aspect of their business single-handedly. This chapter explores the importance of shifting away from this mentality and embracing outsourcing as a strategic tool for business growth and personal freedom.

Throughout this book, we will delve deeper into the following topics. But for now, I want to scratch the surface with some of the key concepts that will help you develop the mindset that will enable you to effectively and efficiently outsource.

Overcoming the Do-It-All Mentality

The belief that one must do all the work personally stems from a combination of pride, fear, and a misunderstanding of cost-effectiveness. It's a common misconception that handling everything yourself saves money. However, this approach often leads to burnout, stagnation in business growth, and a significant opportunity cost. When you're tangled up in day-to-day tasks, you're not focusing on strategic planning and growth activities.

Embracing the Outsourcing Mindset

An outsourcing mindset involves recognizing that delegating tasks can be more efficient and beneficial for your business. It's understanding that your time has value and that by outsourcing certain tasks, you can focus on areas where you add the most value. This mindset isn't just about getting work done; it's about optimizing *how work gets done.*

Benefits of an Outsourcing Mindset

One of the key benefits of outsourcing is increased productivity and efficiency. That's because outsourcing allows you to tap into specialized skills and expertise, leading to higher quality work getting done in less time.

Focus on Core Activities

Outsourcing allows you to delegate peripheral tasks and concentrate on core business activities like strategy, growth, and innovation.

Scalability

Scalability is another major benefit of outsourcing since outsourcing provides you with the flexibility to scale your business operations up or down without the constraints of in-house resources.

Improved Work-Life Balance

And let's not overlook the improved work-life balance that outsourcing offers. Delegating tasks frees up your time, allowing you to enjoy life more fully – be it spending time with family, indulging in hobbies, traveling, or simply relaxing.

How to Develop an Outsourcing Mindset

If you truly want to develop an outsourcing mindset, it's imperative that you acknowledge the value of your time. You start this by literally evaluating the worth of your time. If a task can be outsourced at a lower cost than your hourly rate, it makes financial sense to outsource it.

Identify Tasks to Outsource

Make a list of time-consuming tasks that don't necessarily require your personal expertise. These could include administrative tasks, customer service, or even certain aspects of marketing.

Always Start Small

Begin by outsourcing smaller tasks. This will help you get comfortable with the process and see the benefits firsthand.

Choose the Right Freelancers for Your Team

Invest time in finding the right freelancers who align with your business values and have the necessary expertise.

Embrace Continuous Learning

Stay open to learning and adapting. The world of outsourcing is dynamic, and staying informed will help you make better decisions.

The Bigger Picture

Developing an outsourcing mindset is not just about improving business efficiency; it's about creating a lifestyle that aligns with your personal and professional goals. It's about building a business that supports your life, not one that consumes it. By embracing this mindset, you set the stage for not only business success but also personal fulfillment.

Remember, outsourcing is not a sign of weakness or inability. It's a strategic approach that some of the most successful businesses and entrepreneurs worldwide use. By shifting your mindset and embracing the power of outsourcing, you open doors to new possibilities, growth, and a balanced life.

In essence, developing an outsourcing mindset is about recognizing the value of your time and the potential of your business. It's about making strategic choices that propel both your business and personal life toward your desired goals and visions.

Chapter 2: What Is Outsourcing?

Grasping the Essence of Outsourcing

Let me start by explaining exactly what is outsourcing. Picture this: instead of juggling every task in your business, you hand over some tasks to experts outside your company. That, in a nutshell, is outsourcing. It's like saying, "Hey, I might not be the best at this particular thing, so I'll let someone else handle it." By doing so, you're tapping into external talents and services rather than trying to do everything independently.

Drawing the Line: Outsourcing vs. In-House Hiring

Now, let's differentiate between outsourcing and in-house hiring. Imagine you're throwing a party. Hiring in-house is like having a full-time chef in your home, preparing meals every day. They use your kitchen, follow your house rules, and you oversee their work directly. On the other hand, outsourcing is like hiring a caterer for the event. They come, serve the food, and leave. They have their own tools, work on their terms, and you don't need to watch over them constantly. The caterer isn't part of your household, but they get the job done, often with a flair you might not have achieved on your own.

In the business realm, when you hire in-house, you're bringing someone into your company's fold. They're on your payroll, benefit from your company perks, and are immersed in your company culture. Outsourcing, however, is a different ball game. You're essentially telling another company or freelancer, "I trust you to handle this for me." They're not your employees. They are more like your partners for a specific task or duration.

Diving Deeper: The Two Faces of Outsourcing
1. Offshoring:

Think of offshoring as a hybrid form of outsourcing and in-house hiring. With offshoring, it's all about sending tasks overseas, usually to places where the cost of labor is friendlier on the wallet. So, if your small business is a tech start-up in the U.S., you might have your customer support team working in a bustling Indian city. With offshoring, the workers are normally part-time or sometimes even full-time employees of your business as opposed to independent contractors. Although you may consider them part-time or full-time employees, it is not necessary for you to provide the same benefits to them that you would provide to someone who you hired to work in-house. Offshoring is cost-effective, but remember, it's not always smooth sailing. Time zones can be tricky, and cultural nuances might throw you a curveball now and then.

2. Freelancing:

And now we enter the realm of another source of outsourcing: The world of freelancing – it's dynamic, diverse, and oh-so-flexible. Freelancers are those savvy individuals who've decided to offer their skills on a project-by-project basis. They're not tied down, and with platforms like Upwork and Fiverr, they're just a click away. Need a logo? There's a freelancer for that. A blog post? Yes, there's one for that too. They bring expertise without the long-term commitment, allowing you to scale your operations based on your ever-changing needs.

To wrap things up, whether you use offshoring or freelancing, the labels are not important. What's of utmost importance is that you understand that outsourcing can be like a Swiss Army knife for your business. It's versatile, practical, and can be a game-changer when used correctly. Whether you're venturing into offshoring or freelancing, each has its unique flavor and set of challenges. But remember, it's all about finding the right fit for your business puzzle. So, next time you're feeling swamped, maybe it's time to give outsourcing a shot. After all, why do everything yourself when a world of talent is waiting to collaborate?

Chapter 3: The Perks of Outsourcing Is More than Just Cost Savings

1. Cost Savings: The Tip of the Iceberg

Let's start with the obvious. Outsourcing can indeed be a blessing for your company's finances. Think about it: instead of shelling out for full-time salaries, benefits, office space, and training, you only pay for the specific services you need. It's like dining à la carte instead of splurging on a lavish buffet you might not fully consume. By tapping into regions with lower operational costs, you can get quality work without the hefty price tag. But remember, while saving money is great, it's just one slice of the outsourcing pie.

2. Access to Specialized Skills: The Experts' Playground

Have you ever tried fixing a leaky faucet with no plumbing experience? It can be a wet and wild mess. Similarly, not every task in your business is within your team's expertise. Enter outsourcing. It's like having a Rolodex of experts at your fingertips. Need a cutting-edge website? There's a web development agency for that. Need a mobile app that functions on both Android and IOS? There's a mobile app development team for that, too. Or how about a market research deep dive? A specialized firm is ready to dive in. Outsourcing allows you to tap into a vast pool of experts who live and breathe their specialties. No more makeshift solutions or "learning on the job." You get top-notch quality from professionals who know their stuff. And these experts can be working while you're fast asleep.

3. Flexibility: The Business Gymnast

Business isn't always predictable. There are peak seasons, project influxes, and unexpected lulls. Hiring an in-house full-time team for fluctuating demands can be like buying a 10-bedroom mansion for a family of three – overkill. Outsourcing offers the flexibility to scale up or down based on your current needs. It's like having an expandable house that adapts to your requirements. Need extra hands during the holiday rush? Contract them. When things slow down, scale back without the heartache of layoffs or underutilized staff.

4. Focusing on Core Business Functions: Keeping Your Eye on the Prize

Imagine you're a renowned chef, but instead of crafting culinary masterpieces, you're bogged down with accounting, supply chain issues, and managing reservations. Sounds chaotic, right? In business, it's essential to focus on what you do best and let others handle the rest. Outsourcing allows you to zero in on your core competencies – the things that make your business unique. By delegating peripheral tasks, you can channel your energy and resources into driving growth, innovation, and delivering unparalleled value to your customers. Outsourcing allows you to concentrate on efforts that will move the needle for your business, such as strategizing.

5. Speed and Efficiency: The Fast Track to Success

In the fast-paced world of business, time is of the essence. Waiting around to recruit, train, and onboard a team can be a painstakingly slow process. Outsourcing is like hopping on an express train. You get immediate access to experienced professionals ready to hit the ground running. Whether it's launching a marketing campaign or rolling out a new product, outsourcing can significantly reduce your time to market.

6. Risk Management: Sharing the Load

Every business venture comes with its fair share of risks. Whether it's market fluctuations, technological disruptions, or regulatory changes, the business landscape is ever-evolving. Outsourcing allows you to share these risks with your freelancers. They bring their industry insights, expertise, and risk management strategies to the table, helping you navigate the choppy waters of uncertainty.

7. Continuous Improvement: The Learning Curve

Freelancers are in the thick of their respective fields. They constantly update their skills, tools, and methodologies to stay competitive. By collaborating with them, you indirectly benefit from this continuous learning and improvement. It's like having a personal trainer who's always up-to-date with the latest fitness trends, ensuring you get the best workout possible.

8. Global Reach: Expanding Horizons

Outsourcing can be your ticket to global markets. By working with freelancers in different regions, you gain insights into local cultures, consumer behaviors, and market dynamics. It's like having a local guide when you're traveling, showing you the hidden gems and nuances of the area.

9. Time Freedom

Outsourcing allows you to get your life back. As I mentioned earlier, when I started using outsourcing in my business, it freed up my time to spend more time with my family, devote more time to my hobbies, travel, and live life on my own terms instead of being chained down to my business. With outsourcing, I don't have to spend time doing tasks I don't like, such as responding to customer help desk tickets or creating YouTube thumbnail images.

In wrapping up, outsourcing is more than just a cost-saving strategy. It's a multifaceted tool that offers a plethora of benefits, from specialized expertise and flexibility to risk management and global reach. So, the next time someone mentions outsourcing, remember: it's not just about the money – it's about harnessing a world of opportunities to elevate your business to new heights.

Chapter 4: Common Objections to Outsourcing

Isn't Outsourcing Expensive?

As a successful business owner, I understand the reservations and uncertainties that come with the decision to outsource. It's a common belief that outsourcing is an expensive endeavor and that paying others for tasks you can do yourself is not cost-effective. This perspective is entirely logical, but it's a mindset that needs to be reevaluated if you're aiming for rapid and significant growth in your business.

In my early days, I grappled with this very issue. I believed that by doing everything myself, I was saving money. However, this approach became a major impediment to my business's growth. Over time, I realized that outsourcing is not just about spending money to have someone else do the work; it's about strategically investing in your business's future.

Let's address the concern about cost. Outsourcing can indeed seem expensive at first glance. But, when you analyze the long-term benefits and the efficiency it brings, it often turns out to be a cost-effective solution. It's not merely a transactional expense but an investment in freeing up your time and resources to focus on the core aspects of your business that drive growth and revenue.

Consider the value of your time as an entrepreneur. It is, without a doubt, your most precious asset. By outsourcing tasks, you're essentially buying time – time that can be better spent on strategic planning, business development, networking, or even personal rejuvenation, which is crucial for maintaining your creativity and drive.

Moreover, outsourcing opens the door to specialized skills

and expertise that might not exist within your current team. This can lead to higher-quality outcomes and innovation. Ultimately benefiting your business. Yes, a skilled freelancer might come at a higher cost, but their expertise can add immense value that far exceeds the cost of their services.

Another important aspect to consider is scalability. As your business grows, the ability to scale operations quickly and efficiently becomes vital. Outsourcing provides the flexibility to scale your workforce up or down based on your business needs without the long-term commitments and overheads associated with hiring full-time employees.

Furthermore, by outsourcing, you're not just hiring a service; you're also potentially gaining a partner who can bring in fresh perspectives and ideas to your business. This collaborative approach can lead to innovative solutions and strategies, pushing your business towards new horizons.

While outsourcing might appear costly initially, its true value lies in the return on investment it offers in terms of time, quality, flexibility, and innovation. Shifting your perspective from seeing outsourcing as an expense to viewing it as a strategic investment is crucial. Once I embraced this mindset, the growth and success of my business accelerated significantly. I encourage you to consider outsourcing not just as a means to delegate tasks but as an integral part of your business strategy to drive growth and success.

As someone who has navigated the challenging waters of building a business while juggling other commitments, I understand the dilemma of valuing one's time versus the cost of outsourcing. Let me share an example to put this into perspective, one that I often reflect upon from my own journey.

Imagine you're working a full-time job with an annual salary of $100,000. You work 50 weeks a year, clocking in 40 hours each week. Breaking it down, that's $2,000 per week. Divide that by the 40 hours you work, and your hourly wage is $50.

Now, consider this scenario: you're passionately building an online business in your spare time. The goal is growth, but time is a limited resource. If you find yourself in a position where you can hire skilled talent for, let's say, about $5 an hour, and you know your own professional time is worth $50 an hour, it's a clear mismatch to spend your valuable time on tasks that can be outsourced at a much lower rate.

Yes, it's true that hiring someone is an additional expense. However, this is where strategic thinking comes into play. By investing in outsourcing, you're effectively buying time that can be redirected towards scaling your business, strategizing, or even enhancing your product or service. This approach isn't just about cost-saving; it's about value-adding.

In the early stages of my business, I faced the same crossroads. The realization that my time could be better spent on high-impact activities rather than tasks that could be efficiently handled by someone else was a game-changer. It's about recognizing that your time is a valuable asset and should be allocated with the highest return on investment.

Outsourcing isn't just a financial decision; it's a strategic move towards efficiency and growth. When you calculate the value of your time versus the cost of outsourcing, the math often leans in favor of delegation. By doing so, you're not only leveraging your resources more effectively but also accelerating the growth trajectory of your business. You're giving yourself the bandwidth to focus on big-picture thinking, innovation, and driving your business forward.

To encapsulate, embracing outsourcing as a key component of your business strategy is a testament to understanding the true value of your time and expertise. It's a step towards working smarter, not just harder, and a commitment to the growth and success of your venture. As I mentioned earlier, as a business owner, this mindset shift was instrumental in my journey, allowing me to scale my business while maintaining a balance with other personal and professional commitments.

Doesn't Outsourcing Mean Losing Control of Your Business?

As an experienced business owner, I've often encountered the argument that outsourcing means losing control over your business. Let me offer a different perspective, one that has been instrumental in my own journey of growth and success.

To truly expand and evolve your business at an optimal pace, it's essential to embrace the art of delegation. This often means relinquishing some level of control, allowing others to step in and handle various tasks. Initially, this can feel counterintuitive, especially when you've built your business from the ground up. But the reality is that effective outsourcing is not about losing control; it's about strategically distributing control to enhance efficiency and productivity.

In the realm of outsourcing, you have the opportunity not just to find individuals who can perform a task as well as you can but often find those who can do it even better. Their expertise and specialized skills can bring a new level of quality and innovation to your business.

Consider this scenario: You come across freelancers who excel in a particular task or job, a task that's necessary for your business but not necessarily within your wheelhouse of expertise. These freelancers are not only more skilled in that specific area but also offer their services at a rate that's lower than your own hourly value. In such cases, hiring them is not a no-brainer choice; it's a strategic business decision.

By outsourcing to these skilled individuals, you're not just delegating tasks. You're enabling your business to grow more rapidly than if you juggle everything alone. It's about playing to your strengths and allowing others to contribute their expertise where it's most needed. This doesn't mean you're relinquishing your vision or direction for the business. Rather, you're enhancing it by bringing in the right people to complement your vision.

Moreover, outsourcing opens up your schedule, allowing you

to focus on areas where your impact is most significant—be it strategy, business development, or innovation. This shift in focus from working in your business to working on your business is a critical transition every successful entrepreneur must navigate.

In my experience, the transition to effective outsourcing involved a mindset shift. It required recognizing that control is not about micromanaging every aspect of the business but about steering it in the right direction by leveraging the best resources available. It's about understanding that the most successful leaders are those who recognize their limitations and are not afraid to seek expertise from others.

While some may view outsourcing as a loss of control, I see it as a strategic realignment of resources. It's about empowering your business with the right mix of skills and expertise, ensuring it thrives and grows in a competitive marketplace. Remember, the goal is not to do everything yourself but to ensure everything necessary for your business's growth is done effectively, whether by you or through skilled outsourcing.

If Someone Is Not In-House, Won't Your Instructions Be Misunderstood?

In my years as a business owner, one lesson stands out starkly: the absolute necessity of providing your freelancers with clear, precise instructions. Think of clarity in communication as the golden key in the business world. It's akin to a reliable GPS in a car; without it, you'll likely find yourself wandering in a confusing landscape of misinterpretations and errors.

Imagine your set of instructions as a well-curated recipe book. Sure, an experienced chef can rustle up a meal without a recipe, but a recipe ensures that every dish maintains a consistent quality and taste. It's a blueprint for success. In this book, I'll guide you through some excellent tools and techniques for creating these 'recipes' or templates for instructions, making your life considerably easier.

When conveying these instructions to your freelancers, written text is often a reliable method. It's clear, easily accessible, and serves as a reference point that can be revisited as needed. However, it's important to recognize the power of visual aids. Sometimes, a video demonstration can be vastly more effective than written instructions. It's similar to the difference between reading a manual on how to tie a tie and actually watching someone do it – each method serves its purpose, but one may be more suitable than the other, depending on the context.

For complex or nuanced tasks, visual aids like videos or diagrams can provide a level of clarity that text alone might not achieve. They help bridge any gaps in understanding, especially when dealing with intricate processes or when your freelancer is from a different cultural or linguistic background.

In addition, consider using project management tools where you can integrate both written and visual instructions, along with real-time feedback and queries. This not only enhances understanding but also fosters a collaborative environment where your freelancer feels supported and clear about expectations.

Another aspect that cannot be overlooked is the importance of regular check-ins. These provide an opportunity to clarify doubts, adjust the instructions if necessary, and ensure everyone is aligned with the project's goals. It's about creating a dynamic workflow where communication flows freely, and adjustments can be made swiftly.

In summary, if you use the proper techniques and tools to provide your freelancers with instructions, there wouldn't be any greater reason for the instructions to be misunderstood than if you were giving instructions to in-house employees. The key to a successful outsourcing partnership is effectively communicating your expectations and instructions. Whether through written guidelines, visual demonstrations, or interactive project management tools, ensuring clarity in your communication will save you time and resources and lead to better outcomes. As you progress through this book, I'll introduce more strategies and tools to refine this process, helping you to build a streamlined, efficient, and productive working relationship with your freelancers.

So, I hope that in this chapter, I've clarified that most communication hiccups stem from unclear instructions. It's like trying to assemble a puzzle without the picture on the box. If you can master the art of producing crystal-clear instructions, you'll sidestep a majority of potential miscommunications. It's that simple. And just so you know, I'm not leaving you to figure this all out alone. In this book, I'll uncover a treasure trove of tips, techniques, and tools to help you expand your business's growth through outsourcing.

Chapter 5: Navigating the Complexities of Outsourcing

Outsourcing is an increasingly popular strategy for small and home-based businesses looking to expand and thrive in a competitive market. While it opens doors to global talent, cost efficiencies, and a focus on core business activities, it's not without complexities. This chapter delves into the common challenges associated with outsourcing—such as communication barriers, quality control, and security issues—and offers strategic solutions to navigate these waters effectively.

Understanding Communication Barriers

In my experience as a business owner who has extensively leveraged outsourcing, I've learned that effective communication is not just important – it's vital. It's the backbone of any thriving outsourcing relationship. Challenges in this realm are diverse, from language barriers and time zone differences to navigating various cultural nuances. To successfully manage these complexities, a strategic approach is essential.

When selecting freelancers, it's crucial to look beyond their technical capabilities. Yes, their technical expertise is important, but their ability to communicate clearly and effectively is equally vital. Their cultural adaptability and sensitivity can make a significant difference in how smoothly your collaboration goes. It's about finding a partner who can not only do the job but also seamlessly integrate into your workflow and company culture.

After choosing the right outsourcing partner, the next critical step is to establish a solid foundation for communication. This involves setting up robust communication protocols that suit both parties. Regular video conferences using Skype or WhatsApp are invaluable for maintaining a personal connection and ensuring everyone is on the same page. These meetings can foster a sense of team unity and provide a platform for discussing progress, addressing concerns, and brainstorming ideas.

In addition to video calls, detailed email exchanges play a crucial role. They serve as a written record of discussions, decisions, and action items, which is especially useful for reference and clarity. However, emails should be complemented with more dynamic tools.

This is where collaborative project management tools come into play. Platforms like Asana, Trello, or Slack can significantly enhance communication efficiency. They allow for real-time updates, task tracking, and centralizing information, making it easier for everyone to stay informed and engaged regardless of location.

Another key aspect is being mindful of each other's working hours, public holidays, and cultural practices. This demonstrates respect and consideration, fostering a positive working relationship. It's about finding a balance that works for both parties, which may sometimes involve compromise or finding creative solutions to overcome cultural and time zone challenges.

Moreover, effective communication in outsourcing is not just about exchanging information; it's about building a relationship. Take the time to get to know your freelancers. Understand their work environment and what motivates them. This human connection can significantly impact the quality and efficiency of their work.

Lastly, be open to feedback and adapt your communication style if needed. Effective communication is a two-way street, and being receptive to suggestions on how to improve interaction can lead to more productive and harmonious collaborations.

In summary, the success of an outsourcing relationship hinges greatly on how well you communicate. It's about choosing freelancers who are not only skilled in their trade but are also effective communicators and culturally adaptable. Then, it's about building a framework for regular, clear, and respectful communication, taking into account the diverse contexts in which your freelancing partners operate. By prioritizing effective communication, you pave the way for a successful, collaborative, and respectful outsourcing partnership.

Ensuring Quality Control

As someone who has built a successful business with a significant portion of work outsourced, I can attest to the fact that maintaining quality control is one of the most pressing concerns. It's true the thought of entrusting parts of your business to external teams can be unnerving, particularly with the fear of compromised standards. However, with a strategic and systematic approach, these fears can be effectively mitigated, ensuring that the quality of your business outputs remains top-notch.

The first step in this process is to set crystal-clear expectations. This means having a detailed conversation about the scope of work, the quality benchmarks that need to be met, and the deadlines for each task or project. These details should be meticulously outlined in your instructions and, if necessary, in your agreements or contracts. Clarity here is non-negotiable – it eliminates ambiguity and sets a clear roadmap for your freelancers to follow.

But setting expectations is just the start. Regular (but not excessive) monitoring and establishing of feedback loops are crucial to maintaining quality. This involves setting up routine check-ins, perhaps weekly or bi-weekly. Depending on the nature of the work, more frequent check-ins may be a better idea. These check-ins allow you to review progress, provide feedback, and make adjustments as needed. They also serve as an opportunity for your freelancers to raise any concerns or seek clarification, ensuring that everyone is aligned and on track.

I also recommend a phased approach to scaling your outsourcing efforts. Start by assigning smaller, less critical tasks to your new freelancers. This gives you a chance to assess their capabilities and reliability without putting your core business operations at risk. As they demonstrate their competence and the quality of their work, you can gradually increase their responsibilities. This step-by-step process not only builds trust but also establishes a robust quality control process that can be scaled as your business grows.

Additionally, it's important to establish clear milestones within each project. These milestones act as checkpoints where you can assess the quality of work done so far and make any necessary corrections. This approach helps keep the project on track and ensures that any issues are identified and addressed early.

In my journey, I've found that effective communication plays a vital role in quality control. Make sure that your freelancers understand the importance of quality in your business and encourage open communication. If they encounter challenges or foresee potential quality issues, having an environment where they can communicate these openly and promptly can make a significant difference.

Furthermore, consider incorporating quality metrics or KPIs (Key Performance Indicators) into your assessment process. These metrics can provide objective data on your freelancing partners' performance and help make informed decisions about the continuation or adjustment of their services.

In conclusion, quality control in outsourcing is about setting clear expectations, regular monitoring, phased responsibility scaling, effective communication, and using data-driven approaches for assessment. By implementing these strategies, you can ensure that the quality of your business operations remains high, even as you leverage the benefits of outsourcing. Remember, quality control is not just a process; it's a commitment to the standard of excellence your business upholds.

Addressing Security Concerns

If your business or industry involves sensitive data issues, then addressing security concerns is paramount. When you're handing over tasks that involve sensitive data or intellectual property, the stakes are understandably high. It's not just about getting the job done; it's about ensuring the safety and confidentiality of your information.

If your business or industry involves sensitive data issues, the first step in this process is choosing your freelancers with utmost care. It's essential to work with individuals or entities that are not only aware of the data protection standards in your industry but are also actively compliant with them. This isn't just a matter of trust; it's a matter of ensuring they have the necessary protocols and systems in place to safeguard your sensitive data.

Your legal agreements with freelancers should be thorough and clear. Make sure they include non-disclosure clauses that are specifically tailored to the nature of the work and the type of information they will handle. Also, detail the data handling procedures in your contracts. This might seem like a lot of legalese, but it's crucial for setting clear boundaries and expectations regarding data security. With that said, the reality is that a non-disclosure agreement, or any other agreement or contract, is only as strong as the integrity of the parties signing it.

With that in mind, when it comes to sensitive data issues, having your freelancers sign agreements or contracts shouldn't be your only method of safeguarding. Investing in the right technology to ensure secure operations is equally important. Use communication channels that are encrypted and secure file-sharing platforms that offer advanced security features. This adds an extra layer of protection and peace of mind. In today's digital age, cybersecurity is not an option; it's a necessity.

Furthermore, it's crucial to keep your cybersecurity policies up to date. The digital landscape is constantly evolving, with new threats emerging regularly. Regular reviews and updates of your security policies ensure that you stay ahead of potential risks. This also involves ensuring that your freelancers are abreast of these updates and are implementing them diligently.

In addition to these measures, consider conducting regular security audits. These audits can help identify any vulnerabilities in your data protection strategies and provide insights into the security practices of your freelancers. If possible, include clauses in your agreements allowing these periodic audits, ensuring ongoing compliance and vigilance.

It's also worth mentioning the importance of training and awareness. Ensure that your in-house team and freelancers are trained in best practices for data security. Regular training sessions on the latest security threats and how to avoid them can go a long way in safeguarding your business's sensitive information.

In my experience, addressing security concerns in outsourcing is about creating a culture of security and vigilance. It's a combination of choosing the right freelancers, drafting detailed legal agreements, investing in secure technology, regularly updating your policies, conducting audits, and fostering ongoing awareness. By taking these steps, you can significantly mitigate the risks associated with outsourcing and create a secure environment for your business operations.

Strategies for Risk Mitigation

Mitigating the risks associated with outsourcing is not just a necessary step but a strategic one. The process begins well before you even sign a contract; it starts with carefully vetting potential freelancers or "outsourcing partners," as I like to refer to them. Look for those who not only have a proven track record and positive client feedback but also exhibit a readiness to align with your business's values and standards. It's about finding a synergy between their capabilities and your business needs.

Once you've selected your outsourcing partners, the next step is to cultivate a strong, collaborative relationship with them. This is something I've always emphasized in my business dealings. Treat your outsourcing partners as if they are an integral part of your team, not just external contributors. Involve them in relevant business discussions, keep them in the loop about your company's vision and goals, and, most importantly, acknowledge and appreciate their contributions. This approach not only builds loyalty but also encourages them to have a vested interest in the success of your business. When they understand and connect with your objectives, their commitment to delivering quality work increases.

But even with the best freelancers and strategies in place, the business world is unpredictable. That's why having a contingency plan is non-negotiable. The dynamic nature of business means that unforeseen circumstances can and do arise. Whether it's market shifts, technological changes, or even issues with your freelancers, you need to be prepared. This preparation could involve having a list of backup providers or retaining certain capabilities in-house. It's about ensuring that no single point of failure can significantly disrupt your business operations.

Another aspect of risk mitigation is regular performance reviews and open communication. Set up a system where you regularly assess the performance of your outsourcing partners. This helps in identifying areas where they excel and areas that may need improvement. Open communication about these assessments can lead to constructive discussions and proactive solutions to any emerging issues.

Also, stay informed about the latest trends and changes in your industry and ensure your outsourcing partners are equally informed. This ongoing education can help you both stay ahead of potential risks and capitalize on new opportunities.

In addition, legal compliance and understanding the legal implications of outsourcing are crucial. If you have an outsourcing partner leave a freelancer platform to work for you exclusively, make sure your contracts are comprehensive and cover all aspects of the partnership, including confidentiality, data protection, and intellectual property rights. This legal groundwork may save you from many potential headaches down the line.

To clarify, mitigating risks in outsourcing is about a combination of careful outsourcing partner selection, fostering strong relationships, being prepared for the unexpected, maintaining open communication, staying informed, and ensuring legal compliance. By adopting this multi-faceted approach, you can navigate the complexities of outsourcing, turning potential risks into opportunities for growth and success.

Beyond the Basics: Advanced Considerations

I've come to understand that there's much more to outsourcing than just the basics. When you're ready to scale up your outsourcing efforts, it's essential to consider the broader, long-term implications of these decisions. One strategy I've found particularly effective is adopting a multi-vendor approach. This means diversifying your outsourcing by working with multiple providers. The advantage here is twofold: it reduces your dependency on any single provider and helps mitigate risks. If one vendor encounters a problem, your operations aren't left in a lurch.

However, simply diversifying your outsourcing portfolio isn't enough. Staying informed about market trends and technological advancements is equally important. This knowledge can give your business a competitive edge. It allows you to adapt quickly to changes in the market and take advantage of new technologies and methodologies that could enhance your business operations.

Another key area to focus on is the training and development of both your in-house team and your outsourcing partners. In a rapidly evolving business landscape, ensuring that everyone involved in your business is up-to-date with the latest industry practices and technologies is crucial. This not only leads to improved efficiency but also fosters innovation. Regular training sessions, webinars, or informal knowledge-sharing meetups can be highly beneficial. Remember, an informed team is an empowered team.

Regular assessment of your outsourcing arrangements is also vital. This goes beyond merely looking at the quality of work being delivered. It's about evaluating the overall impact of these outsourcing efforts on your business. Are they aligning with and contributing to your business goals? Is the return on investment what you expected? These regular assessments are more than just a health check; they're a strategic tool that guides you in making informed decisions about the direction of your outsourcing strategy.

In these evaluations, consider not just the financial aspects but also the value addition in terms of innovation, time saved, and market responsiveness. Sometimes, the benefits of outsourcing are not immediately visible in the balance sheet but are evident in the long-term growth and stability of your business.

Also, be open to feedback from both your in-house team and outsourcing partners. Their insights can provide valuable perspectives that can help refine your outsourcing strategies further. It's important to create a culture where feedback is encouraged and valued.

Finally, consider the scalability and flexibility of your outsourcing arrangements. As your business grows, your needs will evolve. Your outsourcing strategies should be able to adapt to these changes. This might mean renegotiating contracts, exploring new outsourcing partnerships, or bringing some previously outsourced functions back in-house.

In essence, when scaling up your outsourcing efforts, it's about looking at the bigger picture and planning for the long term. It's a balance of strategic diversification, staying informed, continuous learning, regular assessment, and adaptability. This comprehensive approach ensures that your outsourcing efforts not only support your current business needs but are also aligned with your future growth plans.

In conclusion, while there are plenty of challenges and complexities to navigate in outsourcing, they can be skillfully managed and even turned into opportunities. By adopting a strategic approach, maintaining clear communication, and nurturing strong partnerships, outsourcing can become an invaluable asset in the growth and scalability of your small business. Remember, successful outsourcing is about more than just delegating tasks—it's about building relationships that foster mutual growth and prosperity.

Chapter 6: Cultural and Time Zone Differences in Outsourcing

Outsourcing is a gateway to a world of diverse talents and perspectives. However, this diversity brings its own set of challenges, particularly when it comes to cultural and time zone differences. This chapter explores these challenges and offers practical strategies to bridge these gaps, fostering a harmonious and productive working relationship.

Navigating Cultural Differences

Every culture has its own set of values, communication styles, and work ethics, which can significantly influence business interactions. When these cultural differences are not acknowledged or respected, they can lead to misunderstandings, frustration, and decreased productivity.

To navigate these cultural waters effectively, start by investing time in understanding your outsourcing partners' cultural norms and business etiquette. This doesn't mean becoming an expert in their culture but rather gaining a basic understanding of their values and communication styles. For example, some cultures may value direct communication, while others prefer a more indirect approach. Understanding these nuances can greatly improve interactions.

Encourage cultural sensitivity within your team. Organize training sessions that highlight the importance of cultural awareness. This can help in creating an inclusive environment where differences are not just tolerated but valued.

Overcoming Time Zone Challenges

Working across different time zones presents another layer of complexity. It can lead to delays in communication and project timelines, affecting the overall efficiency of your business operations.

One effective strategy to manage this is by establishing overlapping working hours. Even if it's just for an hour or two, having a set time each day when both teams are available can be invaluable for real-time communication and collaboration.

Technology can also be a great enabler in this regard. Utilize project management tools that allow asynchronous communication and collaboration. This way, despite the time difference, team members can update their progress, leave feedback, and stay connected.

Building Bridges

Building a strong, cohesive team that transcends cultural and time zone barriers requires a deliberate effort. Here are some strategies to foster a more harmonious working environment:

Regular Team Meetings: Schedule regular video conferences that are convenient for all time zones involved. Use this time not just for project updates but also for team-building activities.

Clear Communication: Be clear and concise in your communication to avoid misunderstandings. Use written formats for important instructions or feedback to ensure clarity.

Flexible Work Arrangements: Be flexible with your team's work hours. Flexibility can help accommodate different time zones and also show respect for your team's local commitments.

Celebrate Diversity: Encourage your team to share their cultural backgrounds and local practices. This not only builds understanding but also creates a more engaged and connected team.

Long-Term Strategies

For long-term success, consider these additional strategies:

Cultural Liaisons: Appoint or hire team members who can act as cultural liaisons. These individuals can help bridge cultural gaps and facilitate better understanding among team members.

Feedback Mechanisms: Establish mechanisms for regular feedback from your team about the challenges they face related to cultural or time zone differences. Use this feedback to make continuous improvements.

Cultural Exchange Programs: If resources allow, consider cultural exchange programs where team members get an opportunity to visit and work from the other team's location. This can be a powerful way to build empathy and understanding.

Embracing the diversity that comes with outsourcing can transform these challenges into opportunities for growth and innovation. By understanding and respecting cultural differences, aligning work across time zones, and fostering an inclusive environment, you can leverage the full potential of your global team. Remember, the goal is not just to work across boundaries but to erase them, creating a unified team that drives your business forward.

Chapter 7: Legal and Contractual Considerations in Outsourcing

As you venture into the world of outsourcing to grow and scale your small or home-based business, navigating the legal and contractual landscape becomes paramount. This chapter delves into critical aspects like intellectual property rights, confidentiality agreements, and dispute resolution mechanisms. These components are crucial for safeguarding your business interests and ensuring a smooth collaboration with your outsourcing partners.

Major freelancing platforms have their own agreements. For example, Upwork's default agreement states that whoever pays for the work owns it and that if a client and freelancer want to arrange otherwise, they can create their own contract that supersedes Upwork's default agreement. The information covered in this chapter mainly relates to outsourcing partners who leave the platform where the two of you initially met and intend to work for your business in either a part-time or full-time capacity.

Intellectual Property Rights

Intellectual property (IP) is a key asset for many businesses, especially those in creative, technological, or innovative fields. When outsourcing, the question of who owns the IP for the work created can become complex. Clear stipulations in the contract regarding IP ownership are essential. Typically, you would want to ensure that any work created for your business is your property. However, this needs to be explicitly stated in the contract to avoid any ambiguity.

In some cases, your outsourcing partner may use their own tools or processes that they have developed. In such instances, the contract should clarify the usage rights of these tools both during and after the completion of the project.

Confidentiality Agreements

Confidentiality is another cornerstone in outsourcing agreements. Your business's confidential information, whether customer data, trade secrets, or business strategies, must be protected. A robust confidentiality or non-disclosure agreement (NDA) is indispensable. This agreement should clearly define what constitutes confidential information and the obligations of the outsourcing partner in protecting this information.

Ensure that the NDA covers aspects like the duration of confidentiality, permissible use of information, and protocol in case of any data breaches. It's equally important to remember that different countries have different laws regarding data protection and confidentiality, so the contract should comply with these laws.

Dispute Resolution Mechanisms

Despite the best efforts, disputes can arise in any business relationship. Having a predefined mechanism for dispute resolution in your outsourcing contract can save both time and resources. Decide on the jurisdiction that will govern the contract and specify this in the agreement.

Include clauses that detail the steps to be taken in case of a dispute. These can range from mediation and arbitration to legal proceedings. Mediation and arbitration are often preferred as they are quicker and less costly than going to court.

Practical Tips for Contract Drafting

Drafting an outsourcing contract that covers all legal and contractual aspects requires careful consideration. Here are some practical tips:

Be Specific: Clearly define the scope of work, deliverables, timelines, and payment terms. The more specific the contract, the less room there is for misunderstandings.

Flexibility: While it's important to be specific, also build some flexibility to accommodate changes in business needs or unforeseen circumstances.

Regular Reviews: Laws and business environments are dynamic. Regularly review and update your contracts to reflect any changes in laws, business practices, or your own business strategy.

Legal Expertise: Consider consulting with a legal professional, especially one specializing in outsourcing or international contracts, to ensure your agreement is comprehensive and legally sound.

In summary, understanding and meticulously crafting the legal and contractual aspects of outsourcing arrangements is vital for the protection and success of your business. Paying attention to intellectual property rights, confidentiality, and dispute resolution can prevent future complications, ensuring a mutually beneficial and legally sound relationship with your outsourcing partners. Always remember, a well-drafted contract is not just a legal necessity but a foundation for a strong and secure business partnership. But as a reminder, and I cannot overstress this: An agreement or contract is only as strong as the integrity of the parties signing it.

Chapter 8: What Should You Outsource?

Deciphering the Outsourcing Puzzle: What Should You Hand Over?

It's finally time for us to get down to the nitty-gritty of outsourcing. Let's dive into one of the most crucial aspects of outsourcing: figuring out what to hand off. It's like decluttering your closet. You don't want to toss out your favorite jacket, but do you need ten nearly identical white shirts? Similarly, in the business realm, it's essential to discern which tasks are core to your identity and which can be entrusted to external experts. Let's break this down step by step.

1. The Repetitive Tasks: The Business Hamster Wheel

You know those tasks that keep coming back, day in and day out? They're like that one catchy song that gets stuck in your head – repetitive and, after a while, a tad monotonous. Data entry, invoicing, and basic customer support queries – these are tasks that, while essential, can take up a significant chunk of your team's time.

Outsourcing these repetitive tasks is akin to setting your business on autopilot for certain functions. It ensures that the wheels keep turning without your direct intervention, freeing up your team to focus on more strategic, value-added activities. Plus, specialized outsourcing firms often have the tools and expertise to do these tasks more efficiently.

2. The Specialized Roles: Tapping into Niche Expertise

Imagine you're trying to bake a soufflé for the first time. You could wing it and hope for the best, or you could bring in a seasoned pastry chef to guide you. In the business world, some roles require niche expertise – think IT security, digital marketing analytics, or legal compliance. These aren't just tasks; they're specialized fields of their own.

Outsourcing these roles is like having a direct line to industry experts. Instead of investing in training an in-house team or diving into a field you're unfamiliar with, you can leverage the deep knowledge of professionals who live and breathe these specialties. It's not just about getting the job done; it's about achieving excellence.

3. Short-Term Projects: The Business Sprints

Every now and then, a project pops up that's important but not ongoing. Maybe it's a website redesign, a market research study, or a promotional campaign for a new product launch. These are sprints, not marathons.

Outsourcing short-term projects offers a twofold advantage. First, it saves you from hiring full-time employees for tasks that won't be permanent. Second, it allows you to tap into fresh perspectives. External teams can bring a new set of eyes, offering insights and ideas that might not have surfaced internally.

4. Tasks outside Your Core Competency: Know Your Strengths

Every business has its strengths – the things that set it apart. Maybe it's product innovation, customer relationships, or brand storytelling. These are your crown jewels, the areas where you shine brightest. Then there are the tasks that, while necessary, aren't your forte.

Outsourcing tasks outside your core competency is about playing to your strengths. It's an acknowledgment that while you excel in certain areas, others are best left to those who specialize in them. This approach not only ensures quality but also allows you to double down on what you do best.

5. Cost-Intensive Functions: The Budget Balancers

Let's talk numbers for a moment. Some functions, while essential, can be a drain on your resources. Setting up an entire IT department, for instance, requires significant investment in infrastructure, tools, and continuous training. Outsourcing such functions can be a strategic move to balance the books. You get the expertise without the overhead costs.

6. Writing

If you haven't realized it already, let me make it clear that if there's one thing you should consider outsourcing, it's written content. Even if you're a wordsmith yourself, there's a strong case for handing this task over to professionals. Why? Because it's efficient, and there's a sea of talented writers out there. I remember when I first dipped my toes into outsourcing written content years ago. That in and of itself was an absolute game changer in my business. Instead of spending countless hours writing (and let's be honest now, writing isn't my forte), I had a team producing top-notch content for me. Suddenly, my websites were brimming with quality articles.

When it comes to getting content written, the sky's the limit. Whether you're running a dating website or a blog about tech start-ups, there's a writer out there who's an expert in that niche.

Need a cardiologist to pen an article? Done. How about a tech guru? No problem, amigo.

7. The Beauty of Outsourcing Graphics

The same goes for graphic design. Unless you're a seasoned designer, consider outsourcing your graphics needs. From infographics to logos, there are professionals who can bring your vision to life, allowing you to focus on strategic business moves.

Let's touch on graphics a bit more. Mastering tools like Photoshop or Illustrator isn't everyone's cup of tea. But guess what? There are folks who've spent years honing these skills, and they're just a click away. For instance, we recently outsourced an audiobook cover for an audiobook that we sell on Audible. What was the result? Absolutely stellar. And it didn't break the bank. A young woman from Bangladesh made the audiobook cover for an incredibly affordable price. Another example is an infographic we had designed. While I wouldn't know where to start, our designer delivered a masterpiece in no time. The bottom line? Outsourcing graphics is a smart move, whether you're design-savvy or not.

8. Social Media Management: A Time-Saver

Let's chat about social media. It's a beast of its own. While it's crucial for brand presence, managing it can be a full-time job. The good news? Many tasks can be outsourced. From setting up profiles on platforms like YouTube, Pinterest, or Facebook to daily sharing and commenting – there's an expert for that. Think about the hours you'd save by having someone else handle these tasks. The time you could spend strategizing and growing your business.

9. Coding

It doesn't matter if you're a seasoned software developer or an accomplished mobile app developer; coding is a task that you should outsource. Just because you can do something doesn't mean you should. Sure, you might be a whiz at coding, but is it the best use of your time when you're trying to grow your business? The goal here is to think big and aim high. That means zeroing in on tasks that truly drive your business forward. Writing, coding, and graphic design, while essential, might not be where you should pour all your energy.

10. Conclusion – The Outsourcing Compass

In a nutshell, outsourcing is like having a Swiss Army knife in your business toolkit. It's versatile, efficient, and can be a game-changer. So, if you're on the fence, take the leap because you won't regret it.

But let it remain clear to you that navigating the outsourcing landscape requires a keen sense of direction. It's about discerning which tasks are integral to your business's identity and which can be entrusted to external hands. Remember, outsourcing isn't about offloading tasks haphazardly. It's a strategic decision, one that can free up resources, tap into niche expertise, and drive efficiency.

So, as you stand at the crossroads, pondering what to outsource, let these guidelines be your compass. They'll steer you towards informed decisions that align with your business goals and vision. And who knows? With the right outsourcing choices, the sky's the limit for what your business can achieve.

Chapter 9: What Should You NOT Outsource?

As we dive into the essential topic of "What Should You Not Outsource" in our journey to grow small businesses through outsourcing, it's vital to draw certain boundaries. While outsourcing is a powerful tool for scaling and efficiency, there are areas where caution is paramount. Let's discuss these in detail, keeping in mind that the safety and integrity of your business are non-negotiable.

Guarding the Crown Jewels

The first rule of thumb is to be extremely careful with tasks that demand access to sensitive information or critical business infrastructure. It's akin to safeguarding the most precious assets in your business. For instance, while we might need to grant access to certain tools or accounts, we do so only after thorough vetting and establishing a deep trust. This cautious approach is crucial for platforms where significant financial transactions occur or sensitive customer data is stored. Think of your customer email list, your PayPal account, or your primary email marketing tools – these are the lifelines of your business. A mishap with these can set you back significantly.

Limiting Access: The Safety Net

It's not about completely restricting access but about being judicious in your approach. For example, domain name accounts are critical. They're essentially the digital real estate of your business. Handing over login details should be done sparingly and only when absolutely necessary. If a developer needs access to a specific task, ensure it's for a defined purpose and time.

Harnessing Limited Access Features

Many platforms offer limited access or role-based access features. For instance, in managing our YouTube account, I assign specific roles like "Limited Editor" or "Subtitle Editor." This segmentation of roles allows team members to contribute effectively while safeguarding crucial functionalities. Similarly, platforms like PayPal, Shopify, GoDaddy, and Amazon Seller Central enable you to grant tailored permissions. This allows you to maintain control over critical aspects of your business operations.

Strategic Consideration of Outsourcing Decisions

When deciding what not to outsource, strategic thinking is key. Tasks that are central to your business strategy, involve core competencies or require a deep understanding of your business culture might be better kept in-house. The rationale here is simple: these elements are what set your business apart. They are your competitive edge. For instance, outsourcing your primary product development or core service offering might dilute your brand's unique value proposition.

Building Relationships and Trust Gradually

Trust and strong relationships are the bedrock of successful outsourcing. However, they take time to build. When it comes to tasks that require high levels of trust and confidentiality, start small. Gradually increase the level of responsibility and access as the relationship with the outsourcing partner strengthens. This approach allows you to gauge their reliability and align them with your business values over time.

The Role of NDAs and Legal Agreements

As I mentioned earlier, non-disclosure agreements (NDAs) and robust legal contracts are critical tools in safeguarding your business's sensitive information. But as I stressed earlier, they are not foolproof. However, they add a layer of legal protection and set clear expectations about confidentiality and data handling.

The Bottom Line

Ultimately, the decision between what you should and should not outsource needs to be a balance between the potential gains in efficiency and the need to protect the core integrity of your business. As your business evolves and your relationships with outsourcing partners grow stronger, you can reassess your strategy and make adjustments. Remember, in the world of outsourcing, not everything that can be outsourced should be outsourced. Discernment is key.

Chapter 10: Techniques & Strategies to Determine What to Outsource

Let's dive deep into the art of identifying tasks for outsourcing. Think of this as a strategic game plan to streamline your business operations. Ready? Let's break it down step by step by creating a handful of lists.

List Number 1: The Self-Reflection Phase: Mapping Out Your Day

First things first, let's start with some introspection. Picture your typical workday. From the moment you sit down at your desk, what tasks occupy your time? Let's use a home-based self-publishing business as an example. Your day might involve researching potential book topics, penning down chapters, designing book covers on platforms like Canva, or even running Amazon ads to promote your literary gems. And let's not forget the power of social media. Maybe you're crafting posts for Instagram, Facebook, TikTok, or even uploading videos on YouTube. Whatever fills your day, jot it down. This list is your bird's-eye view of your daily operations.

Time Tracking: Where Do the Hours Go?

Now, with your list in hand, let's play detective. Which of these tasks are the biggest time sinks? Are there any that consume 7 to 10 hours of your week? Mark them and note down the hours you spend on each. If you're juggling your business part-time, pinpoint tasks that take up one or two hours weekly. The idea here isn't to nitpick but to identify areas that, while essential, might not necessarily need your personal touch. Remember, we're brainstorming. Think of this as laying the foundation for a more efficient business model.

List Number 2: The Skillset Inventory: What's in Your Arsenal?

Next up, let's talk about strengths. What are you exceptionally good at? These are tasks that not only align with your business goals but also showcase your expertise. List them. Generally, it's wise to hold onto tasks where you shine, even if they're time-intensive. For instance, if you're a wizard at managing Facebook ad campaigns, it might not make sense to hand over the reins to an agency. Sure, you could consider outsourcing the ad creation part while still overseeing the campaigns. But remember, there's value in your expertise. However, as your business scales, there might come a time when even these tasks could be outsourced for greater efficiency.

The Balancing Act: Merging Passion with Practicality

While it's essential to recognize and nurture your strengths, it's equally crucial to strike a balance. Just because you're great at something doesn't mean it's the best use of your time. As your business grows, you might find that outsourcing certain tasks, even ones you excel at, can free you up to focus on broader strategic goals. Outsourcing is a delicate dance of understanding your business landscape, recognizing your strengths, and making strategic decisions to optimize efficiency. It's not about relinquishing control but about smart delegation. As you navigate this journey, remember to continually reassess and adapt. After all, the business world is ever-evolving, and flexibility is key.

List Number 3: The Revenue-Driving Tasks: Your Business's Pulse

Let's delve into the heart of your business operations with our third list. This one's all about the money-makers: tasks that directly fuel your revenue stream. For the third list, I want you to ask yourself which tasks lead directly to revenue. If a task leads directly to revenue, then even if you were to hate that task, I recommend that you keep doing it, at least in the short term. Try to keep these tasks under your control because they will affect your bottom line at a time when growth is most crucial.

So, for this list, I want you to take a moment and reflect on the tasks that are the lifeblood of your business's financial health. Which activities, when executed, directly translate into dollars and cents? Now, here's the deal: even if some of these tasks aren't your favorite, it's crucial to keep a close eye on them, especially in the initial stages of your business. Why? Because these tasks are the pillars supporting your business's growth. They're the difference between a thriving enterprise and one that's struggling to stay afloat.

Drawing from personal experience with one of my first online ventures, email marketing was our golden goose. It was the primary engine driving our revenue. And even though crafting and managing email campaigns was a time-intensive affair, I chose to handle it personally. Why? Because I recognized its pivotal role in our financial success. If, for instance, your budding business leans heavily on email marketing promotions or Facebook ads as a primary revenue source, it might be wise to keep these tasks close to your chest, at least for the time being. Whether you choose to manage it in-house with a dedicated team or personally take the reins yourself, ensure it's executed with precision and care. So go ahead and list these responsibilities that directly impact your bottom line.

Understanding and closely monitoring your revenue-driving tasks is paramount. It's about safeguarding the financial health of your business and ensuring steady growth. So, as you map out your business strategy, make sure to highlight and prioritize these critical tasks. They're not just tasks; they're the building blocks of your business's success.

List Number 4: The Joy Factor: Doing What You Absolutely Love to Do

For our fourth list, let's start with a simple yet profound question: What do you genuinely enjoy doing? It might seem trivial, but trust me, it's far from it. Imagine a business where you're immersed in tasks you're passionate about while delegating the ones that feel like a chore. Not only does this set the stage for long-term success, but it also contributes to your well-being and happiness as an entrepreneur. If blogging sets your soul on fire, then by all means, keep that pen (or keyboard) in hand. Your passion will resonate with your audience in ways that an outsourced writer might not be able to replicate. It's that unique voice and enthusiasm that can create a genuine connection with your readers.

List Number 5: The "Not My Cup of Tea" List

Now, onto our fifth list. Here, I want you to be brutally honest and list down tasks that make you cringe. If you dread doing something, chances are you might not excel at it. And even if you're decent at it, why spend time on something that drains your energy? For instance, if the mere thought of handling customer support emails gives you a headache, it's a clear sign that this task is for outsourcing.

The Grand Overview: Your Five Lists

Having gone through this introspective exercise, you should now have five distinct lists that provide a comprehensive view of your business tasks:

List Number 1: This captures the tasks that consume most of your time. It's a snapshot of where your hours go.

List Number 2: Here, you've highlighted tasks that you're not just good at but excel in. These are your strengths and areas of expertise.

List Number 3: This list is all about revenue. It pinpoints tasks that directly contribute to your business's bottom line.

List Number 4: This is your "happy place" list, detailing tasks that you genuinely enjoy and look forward to.

List Number 5: On the flip side, this list is a compilation of tasks that you'd rather not touch even with a ten-foot pole.

In conclusion, this exercise aims to strike a balance between efficiency, passion, and practicality. By understanding where your strengths, interests, and aversions lie, you can structure your business in a way that maximizes productivity and personal satisfaction. Remember, a happy entrepreneur is often a successful one. So, as you navigate the complexities of using outsourcing to catapult your business, let these lists be your guiding light, ensuring you stay aligned with your professional goals and personal well-being.

Chapter 11: Crafting Your Outsourcing Blueprint

Let's talk strategy. As a savvy entrepreneur, your ultimate aim is to create a business that thrives, with or without your constant oversight. Imagine the freedom and peace of mind that comes with knowing your venture is ticking along nicely, even when you step away. This isn't just about reducing your stress levels; it's about enhancing the value of your business, enjoying the liberty of free time, and ensuring you have a robust asset that can withstand emergencies or unexpected breaks.

1.) Calculating Your Time's Worth

When funds are tight, the secret to scaling up from where you stand is to figure out your hourly earning rate. That's the value of an hour of your time. Once you've got that number, delegate any task that can be done by someone else for less than it would cost for you to do it yourself. Knowing the worth of your hours gives you a clear-cut way to spot chances for swift growth and eliminate any tasks that are siphoning off your resources more than they should. It's about investing your time wisely and maximizing your financial efficiency.

2.) Begin at Ground Level, Then Elevate

Envision your business as a set of cogs and gears working seamlessly in your absence. That's every entrepreneur's dream, right? But let's not get ahead of ourselves. While it's alluring to dive headfirst into sophisticated project management tools and the latest tech for team communication, simplicity is your ally in the early stages. Start by delegating a handful of tasks. Start out by using straightforward communication channels like email, Skype, or WhatsApp to keep things running smoothly.

The key here is to ease into outsourcing. If you're new to this, assign just a couple of tasks initially. Once you've got a feel for it, gradually introduce more responsibilities. Before you know it, you'll have a well-oiled machine where entire systems operate independently. It's about building confidence and competence, one step at a time.

3.) Initiating Your Outsourcing Journey

Let's get down to brass tacks on how you can start reclaiming your time. You might not be fully aware of which tasks are monopolizing your schedule. A practical first step is to map out all the activities that make up your business routine, noting how often they occur—be it daily, weekly, or monthly. Every business has its peculiarities, and yours might have certain tasks that demand more attention than others.

To pinpoint exactly where your time is going, consider leveraging a tool like RescueTime. It's a free resource that runs quietly in the background, tracking your usage across apps, websites, and software. After a few weeks, it'll serve up a comprehensive report, shining a light on where your hours are being invested. With this data, identify the tasks you're naturally good at or those that bring you joy. These are the tasks you'll want to keep on your plate.

And be mindful of tasks that involve sensitive information—like banking details—which you might prefer to handle personally. Then, there are those time sinks that are more of a headache than they're worth. These should be the first you consider for outsourcing.

Understanding the tasks you're delegating is crucial, especially for recurring ones. Here's why:

- You'll have a ballpark figure of how long tasks should

take, setting realistic expectations.

- When interviewing potential assistants, you can pose informed questions to gauge their expertise.
- You'll have a benchmark for what a completed task should look like, allowing you to assess the quality of work effectively.
- If there's a learning curve, you'll be better equipped to guide your virtual assistant through the process.

Remember, knowledge is power—even when you're passing the baton.

4.) Evaluating Potential Team Members

When considering expanding your team through outsourcing, especially with virtual assistants (VAs), it's wise to approach it with a strategy. Diving headfirst into a full-time commitment can be risky. A more prudent approach is to start on a smaller scale. Assign a clearly defined project – like conducting research on a set number of niches and presenting the findings. This method allows you to gauge not only the quality of their work but also their ability to communicate effectively and adhere to deadlines.

This project-based trial period offers several advantages. Firstly, it provides a real-world evaluation of the VA's skills and working style. You'll get a sense of how well they understand and execute your instructions, their problem-solving abilities, and their attention to detail. Secondly, it lets you assess their reliability. Do they deliver on time? Are they proactive in their communication, especially when encountering challenges?

Another critical aspect to consider is how well they align with your business culture and values. Even if a VA is technically proficient, a mismatch in work ethics or communication style can be a hurdle. This initial project allows you to observe how they fit within the broader context of your business's working environment.

If the VA impresses you with their performance during this trial project, it could be a sign that they're a good fit for your business. At this point, you can consider transitioning to a more regular, hourly arrangement. It's also a good opportunity to discuss expectations for ongoing work, such as availability, communication preferences, and scope of responsibilities.

Remember, the goal of this evaluation period isn't just about finding someone who can complete tasks. It's about finding a team member who can contribute to your business's growth, understands your vision, and works well within your existing team dynamics. Building a strong, cohesive team is crucial for the long-term success of your outsourcing strategy.

In summary, evaluating potential team members, particularly virtual assistants, through a project-based trial is a strategic move. It helps in making informed decisions about their role in your business while minimizing risk. To sum it all up, this approach is not just about assessing their skills but also about understanding how they align with your business's culture and long-term objectives.

5.) Mastering the Art of Delegation

One of the most challenging aspects of business growth for entrepreneurs used to being at the helm of every operation is learning the art of delegation. As someone who has navigated these waters, I can offer some guidance. Embrace the mantra: "Good enough is good enough." Striving for absolute perfection in every task can be a trap. It often leads to stress, inefficiency, and even a sense of demotivation among your team. Instead, the focus should be on the essence of what needs to be achieved.

a.) Outline the Task Clearly: Clearly define what needs to be done. Providing a well-delineated scope helps your team understand the task's parameters and what is expected of them.

b.) Explain the 'Why': Contextualizing the task is crucial. Explain why the task is important and how it fits into the broader goals of the business. This not only ensures clarity but also helps in aligning the team with your vision.

c.) Communicate Non-Negotiables: Every task has its non-negotiables – fundamental aspects that cannot be compromised. Be explicit about these from the outset. This precision helps in setting clear boundaries and expectations.

d.) Step Back and Trust: Perhaps the hardest part is stepping back and trusting your team to deliver. This requires a leap of faith, but it's essential for growth. Remember, delegation is not just about offloading tasks; it's about empowering your team.

As your business grows, it becomes increasingly important to have someone who can manage the nitty-gritty details. Bringing in a team leader or manager can be transformative. This person acts as a bridge between you and your team, handling day-to-day management, problem-solving, and ensuring tasks are on track. Their presence allows you to extract yourself from the minutiae of daily operations, giving you the bandwidth to focus on strategic planning and the bigger picture of your business.

In essence, mastering delegation is about striking a balance between maintaining control and giving autonomy. It's about understanding that while perfection is a noble pursuit, efficiency, and trust are the cornerstones of a thriving business. By effectively delegating, you not only enhance operational efficiency but also foster a culture of trust and empowerment, which are vital for sustainable business growth.

6.) Envisioning the Impact

Let's take a moment to truly envisage the impact of effective outsourcing in your business. Imagine you decide to outsource just 15 hours of work this month. That's effectively like gifting yourself an extra two full workdays. If you extend this practice over a year, you're looking at an additional 22 days. Just think about it – nearly a month's worth of time! This newfound time isn't just empty hours; it's a reservoir of potential. It could be the difference between stagnation and taking your most profitable business aspects to soaring new heights. Or it might be the opportunity for well-deserved relaxation, to rejuvenate and enjoy moments with loved ones, which is just as crucial for a successful entrepreneur.

But the benefits of outsourcing go far beyond mere time-saving. By focusing on strategic process development and team building through outsourcing, you're effectively setting the stage for exponential growth. It's not about inching forward; it's about leaping ahead. Your business's potential could multiply, possibly fivefold or even more. This isn't just speculation – it's a reality I've experienced firsthand. By delegating tasks judiciously, you can maintain or even reduce your current workload, all while your business continues to expand and flourish.

Consider the long-term benefits as well. Outsourcing allows you to tap into a diverse pool of talent and expertise that you might not have had access to otherwise. This diversity can bring fresh perspectives and innovative ideas, propelling your business into new markets or product lines. Additionally, it creates a more agile business model, where scaling up or down in response to market demands becomes smoother and more efficient.

Moreover, outsourcing can be a catalyst for improving internal processes. As you delegate tasks, you're compelled to streamline operations, document procedures, and clarify roles and responsibilities. This exercise often leads to identifying inefficiencies and areas for improvement within your business, leading to a more streamlined and effective operation.

In essence, envisioning the impact of outsourcing is about recognizing its transformative power. With the strategies and insights discussed in this book, you'll be equipped to craft your outsourcing blueprint. And if I haven't already hammered home this point, outsourcing isn't just a tool for managing tasks; it's a strategic approach to business growth, innovation, and personal well-being. As you step out to transform these possibilities into realities, remember that the true value of outsourcing lies in its ability to amplify your business's success and your satisfaction as an entrepreneur.

Chapter 12: The Platforms at Your Disposal

In this vital chapter, we're going to delve into the platforms that form the backbone of successful outsourcing strategies. These platforms have become indispensable tools in my business, and I'm confident they'll be just as invaluable for you. Whether you need to delegate routine tasks or require specialized skills, these are the resources that can make it happen. And in those rare instances where you encounter a highly specialized need, I'll guide you to the niche platforms that can fulfill even the most unique requests. Throughout this section, we'll dissect each platform, offering clear, actionable advice on how to navigate them to your advantage.

Here are the platforms that have become integral to enhancing our business operations:

OnlineJob.ph: This freelancing platform is a treasure trove for recruiting dedicated Filipino professionals. The talent here is not just skilled but also known for a strong work ethic, making it an excellent source for long-term collaborations.

Upwork: This platform is incredibly versatile, offering a gateway to freelancers with diverse skill sets. It's perfect for everything from one-off tasks to long-term projects, providing a wide range of expertise and experience levels.

99 Designs: For design needs, this platform is unmatched. Whether you're seeking a new logo, branding materials, or web design, 99 Designs connects you with creative professionals capable of bringing your vision to life with flair and precision.

Fiverr: When speed is of the essence, and the tasks are well-defined, Fiverr is my go-to. It's perfect for those smaller, quick-turnaround jobs, and the competitive pricing model is a boon for small business budgets.

These platforms aren't just places to find talent; they're ecosystems that support and streamline the outsourcing process. They offer structured environments for communication, payment, and project management, which simplifies the delegation process significantly. With these tools at your disposal, you can expand your team with confidence, knowing that you have access to a global pool of professionals ready to elevate your business operations.

Beyond these, there are specialized platforms for nearly every need. Whether it's coding, writing, analytics, or something else, there's a platform out there that caters to it. Each comes with its own set of benefits and ways of doing things, which we'll explore in depth. My goal is to equip you with the knowledge to use these platforms not just effectively but masterfully.

The beauty of these platforms lies in their flexibility and reach. They've broken down geographic and logistical barriers, enabling businesses like ours to thrive in ways that were unimaginable just a decade ago. With the right approach, these platforms can become a seamless extension of your business, allowing you to delegate tasks confidently and focus on growth.

In the following pages, we'll dive into the specifics of how to maximize the potential of each platform, tailor your searches for the best candidates, and establish processes that ensure smooth project flows and quality results.

These platforms have been instrumental in the scaling of my online businesses, and I'm excited to share the insights and strategies that will help you leverage them for your success. With the detailed guidance provided, you'll be able to navigate the outsourcing world like a seasoned pro.

Chapter 13: OnlineJobs.ph

OnlineJobs.ph, as I mentioned, is a great place to find virtual assistants or even full-time outsourcing staff, just like the other outsourcing platforms that we use. OnlineJobs.ph is very self-explanatory. They do a great job of guiding you through how to find someone, sort through the different applicants, and choose the best one. And it all starts with either posting a job or searching through resumes. You'll communicate with people that you normally find by email. Next, you'll interview them. I recommend that you interview them on Skype or WhatsApp because this way is a lot more thorough than using email. This is also a good way to make sure that the communication is going to be streamlined and seamless.

And again, that's something that can be hard to gauge if you're doing it all through email. People in the Philippines often speak English as a first language, so you can find people who speak perfect English, which is one of the reasons why it's such a great hub for outsourcing. In many of our experiences, the people that you're hiring are sometimes unemployed or between work. So they can start immediately, which is great as far as payments go. The time worked on OnlineJobs.ph can be managed with something called time proof, and you can pay them through Xoom or PayPal or directly from your OnlineJobs.ph account using Easypay.

OnlineJobs.ph is a subscription-based website, but you don't have to subscribe indefinitely. You could subscribe for a month to OnlineJobs.ph while you are finding your assistant or whomever you need, and then you could unsubscribe. You don't have to worry about taxes or anything like that either with OnlineJobs.ph. So, one of the keys in selecting the right person, just like with any of the platforms, is to be very clear and concise in the description and the title.

One of the key things that you look for in applicants is experience with similar jobs they've had in the past. So you want to see that they've got the experience that's required. I always like to find people who have experience, even though initiative or work ethic is just as important. These are the main things that I look for. Again, it's a pretty simple process. Just to make sure that the hiring process on OnlineJob.ph is clear, I've included a 15-step guide. Let's walk through the process together, step by step:

1. Getting Started:

Hop onto OnlineJobs.ph and set up your account. It's pretty straightforward—just fill in the details about you and your business, and you're all set to dive in.

2. Crafting Your Job Post:

Hit the "Post a Job" button and craft a job listing that's clear and enticing. Think of it as a first handshake—you want to be precise about what the job entails and the skills you're after. Don't forget to mention the hours and perks!

3. Resume Hunt:

While you wait for the magic to happen and applications to roll in, take the initiative. Use the search feature to filter through resumes. It's like having a treasure map where you can mark the spots that look promising.

4. Sifting Through Candidates:

As applications come through, take your time to look over each one. OnlineJobs.ph offers an "ID Proof" score to help you spot the genuine gems.

5. The Interview Dance:

Narrow down your list and set up interviews. Whether it's Zoom or Skype, it's your chance to meet face-to-face, virtually speaking. Have your questions ready to get to the heart of their expertise.

6. The Trial Run:

Found some standouts? Give them a test drive with a small, paid task. It's the best way to see them in action and gauge how well they follow through.

7. Reference Checks:

If you can, do a bit of sleuthing with references. A quick chat with past employers can give you peace of mind.

8. Talking Terms:

When you've found 'the one,' it's time to talk shop. Discuss salary, schedules, and set clear expectations. Transparency is key here.

9. Welcome Aboard:

Get your new team member up to speed with all the tools and info they need. A smooth onboarding makes for a happy start.

10. Keep the Lines Open:

Communication is the glue in remote work. Regular updates and open channels keep everyone on the same page.

11. Dot the I's and Cross the T's:

Make sure all the paperwork is in order. Contracts and NDAs are not just formalities—they're your safety net.

12. Payment Procedures:

Figure out the best way to handle payments. OnlineJobs.ph suggests PayPal or Wise for hassle-free transactions. We normally use PayPal.

13. Feedback Loop:

Once they're in the groove, keep an eye on their work and offer feedback. It's about guiding, not micromanaging.

14. Relationship Building:

A good rapport goes a long way. Celebrate the wins and navigate the challenges together.

15. Adapt and Expand:

As your business evolves, so will your needs. Be ready to adjust your team member's role and consider growing your remote team.

And there you have it—a blend of professional insight and friendly advice on how to find and foster a great working relationship with a remote worker through OnlineJobs.ph. Keep it clear, friendly, and professional, and you're on your way to building a solid team.

Chapter 14: Upwork

Upwork.com stands as a premier platform for outsourcing, and it's possibly the one I turn to most frequently among all the resources we've discussed. Like its counterparts, Fiverr and Onlinejobs. ph, Upwork offers an intuitive interface that focuses your efforts on selecting the right candidates rather than navigating the complexities of job postings. The process to post a job is straightforward: you begin by selecting a category and crafting a job title. The trick with the title is to capture the attention of top-tier talent.

Workers are constantly browsing through numerous job listings and are naturally inclined to apply for the ones that stand out. Clarity and conciseness in your title are paramount. You must also articulate the specifics of the job. If the task is time-sensitive, it's crucial to highlight the urgency—this is a tip that's universally applicable across all platforms. For instance, if I require a translation to be completed on the same day, I'll make sure that's evident right from the title or within the job description.

Speaking of the job description, this is where you provide a snapshot of the task at hand and outline the expected deliverables and timeline. It's often prudent to reserve the nitty-gritty details until after you've hired someone, which is a route I frequently take, particularly if the project is complex or contains sensitive information. When setting up the job, you'll choose between a one-time project or an ongoing engagement. Typically, for initial engagements, you'll opt for a one-time project to evaluate the freelancer's work.

Next, you'll input the necessary skills for the job. The more specific you are with the skills—like blog writing or social media content writing—the more likely your posting will reach the appropriate audience. When it comes to visibility settings, you have the option to open your job to all or direct it towards a specific freelancer if you have someone in mind. There might be occasions where you're looking to bring on multiple freelancers; in such cases, you'd adjust the settings accordingly. In the job settings, you'll then define your budget and the desired experience level. Upwork gives you the flexibility to choose between a fixed price or an hourly rate. This choice will depend on the nature of your project and your payment preferences.

When setting up a job on Upwork, I tend to lean towards a fixed price arrangement initially. If you're uncertain about your budget, it's wiser to err on the side of caution and set a lower budget rather than overshooting it. As for the level of experience, I generally advise against opting for entry-level workers since they usually lack substantial experience on the platform. Determining the right price for your job isn't an exact science, but one approach I find useful is to estimate how long the task would take me if I had the necessary skills. For instance, consider the time it would take to write a 500-word blog post about hiring ghostwriters, including the research involved. Then, ask yourself what you're willing to pay per hour for the work.

Alternatively, you can base your budget on the maximum amount you're prepared to spend. It's preferable to start with a lower budget than to set it too high. If the proposals you receive don't meet your expectations, you can always reassess and repost the job.

Fixed rates are typically suited for project-specific tasks such as logo design, content creation, or video editing—tasks where the time required is relatively predictable. However, fixed rates can sometimes incentivize workers to rush through the job to move on to the next one, which might compromise quality. In cases where you want to ensure the work isn't hurried or when the duration of a task is uncertain, an hourly rate may be more appropriate.

For example, when I needed a development team to add features to an existing mobile app, I opted for an hourly rate because I couldn't accurately gauge the time required for the additions. This approach ensures that both parties' expectations are aligned, and with Upwork's timesheet system, the risk of overbilling is minimized.

In the past, there was a concern that freelancers could exploit hourly billing by claiming more hours than they actually worked. However, Upwork has since implemented robust monitoring tools. These tools allow you to track the freelancer's time and ensure that the hours billed reflect the work done. They can log their hours in timesheets, simplifying the payment process if you're paying by the hour.

In summary, Upwork provides features that enable you to track and monitor the actual time freelancers spend on your projects. I highly recommend utilizing these tools to maintain transparency and accountability, ensuring that you get value for the time you're billed.

To sum up everything, here's a guide that will walk you through the entire hiring process at Upwork.

1. **Familiarize Yourself with Upwork**: Get to know the platform's layout and features, such as freelancer categories, job success scores, and rates.

2. **Create a Detailed Job Post**: Draft a job description that includes project scope, required skills, deliverables, and deadlines.

3. **Set a Realistic Budget**: Determine your budget based on the project's complexity and Upwork's market rate suggestions.

4. **Evaluate Proposals**: Review incoming proposals, focusing on the freelancer's cover letter, portfolio, and job history.

5. **Conduct Interviews**: Shortlist candidates and conduct interviews to discuss their experience and approach to your project.

6. **Assess Skills with a Test Job**: For significant

projects, consider a paid test job to evaluate the freelancer's work quality and reliability.

7. **Understand Upwork's Fee Structure**: Be aware of the service fee Upwork charges freelancers, as it may impact their rates.

8. **Use Milestone Payments**: For extended projects, utilize milestone payments to ensure progress and accountability.

9. **Maintain Communication**: Keep in touch with the freelancer throughout the project via Upwork's messaging system.

10. **Provide Feedback**: After project completion, leave feedback for the freelancer, which aids their growth and informs other clients.

11. **Build Relationships**: If satisfied with the work, maintain a relationship with the freelancer for future projects.

12. **Stay Compliant with Terms**: Ensure all interactions and payments adhere to Upwork's terms of service.

13. **Leverage Upwork's Resources**: Take advantage of hiring guides and customer support provided by Upwork.

14. **Be Mindful of Time Zones**: Coordinate with international freelancers considering the differences in time zones.

15. **Secure Intellectual Property**: Use contract templates to protect your intellectual property rights.

16. **Review Work Regularly**: Check the freelancer's submissions periodically to ensure the project stays on course.

17. **Close the Contract Properly**: Once the project is complete, formally close the contract on Upwork and provide feedback.

By systematically following these steps, you can streamline the process of hiring freelancers on Upwork, ensuring a professional and successful collaboration.

Chapter 15: 99Designs

99designs is where creativity meets commerce in a digital marketplace teeming with gifted designers ready to bring your vision to life. These are the steps involved so that you can harness the platform's full potential through design contests and direct collaborations:

1. Reach Out to Designers

Kick things off by inviting designers to your contest. Dive into the Discover tool on 99designs to scout for talent that aligns with your vision. When you spot a designer whose work resonates with you, hit the "Invite to work" button on their profile. This is your chance to engage them with a personal touch. Draft a message that not only invites them to your contest but also acknowledges their work—maybe even highlighting a particular design that caught your eye. Genuine appreciation can be a powerful motivator. It's about making an impression, showing them that you value their unique skills and haven't just blasted out a generic call to action.

Creating a "favorites" list is another strategic move. When I was on the hunt for an illustrative logo, I filtered the search results to zero in on illustrators and then hearted the ones that stood out. When your contest goes live, you'll have a curated list of top picks to invite, saving you time and increasing the chances of finding that perfect match for your project.

2. Navigate the Contest Timeline with Ease

The clock on a standard contest ticks for a week, but don't let the default seven days box you in. If the creative juices need more time to flow, there's no need to rush—extensions are just a support ticket away. Here's how the contest unfolds:

A.) Qualifying Round – This initial phase spans four or six days for web-based contests. It's open season for designers to throw their hats in the ring.

Remember, quality design isn't instant—it's normal for submissions to trickle in over a few days. If the Qualifying Round is winding down and you're still waiting for that 'aha' moment, reach out to the 99designs team. They're on standby to grant you extra time at no cost.

B.) Select Finalists – Now's the time to narrow the field to your top six contenders. This selection marks the transition to the decisive final round.

It's a commitment: Once you've chosen your finalists, the contest is locked in, and refunds are off the table. If you're on the fence about the entries, consider extending the Qualifying Round to explore more options.

C.) Final Round – Over the next three days (or five for web contests), it's just you and your chosen few. There are no new entries here; it's just focused collaboration.

You should be close to the finish line with your finalists, fine-tuning details to get everything just right. If you need a bit more time for those final tweaks, they can stretch this round a bit more for you.

D.) Select Winner/Handover – Choosing your winner is just the beginning. Next is the Handover, where you'll review the final files over five days before the designer's payment goes through.

If things aren't quite perfect, don't hesitate to contact 99Designs support. They can put the auto-payment on hold, ensuring you and the designer have the space to dot the i's and cross the t's.

3. Effective Communication and the Art of Feedback

Engaging with designers by providing feedback isn't just polite—it's the cornerstone of a thriving contest. Clear, constructive comments guide your designers, shaping the evolution of their work to match your vision. Your interaction earns you a feedback score, visible to all designers. It measures your responsiveness and shapes their eagerness to join your contest. A high score draws in talent, while a low one might send them scrolling past. Stay communicative and consistent to keep that score soaring! You can check your rating anytime by hovering over the "You" link on the homepage.

Remember, it's the behind-the-scenes feedback that adjusts your score. To leave your thoughts, click the speech bubble on any design or use the feedback box when viewing an enlarged design.

While public feedback won't nudge your rating, it's still valuable. Drop comments at the bottom of your contest page to broadcast updates to all your contest's creatives.

4. Strategically Use Star Ratings

While it's quite alluring to give a high star rating to a design that catches your eye immediately, pause and ponder the broader implications. Early high ratings can:

- Deter other designers from j\oining the contest, thinking a winner is already a foregone conclusion.
- Lead the highly-rated designer to become complacent, potentially stalling further innovation.
- Spark a trend of similar submissions, as other designers might interpret high ratings as a definitive preference for a particular style.
- Predicting individual reactions to star ratings is a complex affair, but as a rule of thumb, reserve ratings above three stars for designs during the qualifying round that you'd be genuinely content to declare as the winner.

This approach maintains a competitive edge, motivating designers to keep innovating and refining their work. When the final round arrives, and you've narrowed down your top picks, that's the time to liberally distribute those stars!

5. Secure More Talent with a Guaranteed Contest

Consider making your contest guaranteed from the outset. This option becomes available once you enter the Final Round, but if you've previously hosted a successful contest, you can opt to guarantee it right from the start.

You also have the flexibility to guarantee the contest directly from your contest page after receiving ten or more entries. Committing to a guaranteed contest does mean relinquishing the option for a refund, yet it's a powerful incentive that can significantly increase the number of designers eager to participate in your contest. These insights should serve you well as you embark on hosting a design contest.

Chapter 16: Fiverr.com

Fiverr is another platform that I have successfully used to hire freelancers. While I've engaged Fiverr.com for various projects, my preference leans towards Upwork, especially when seeking specialized talent.

However, I've encountered exceptions to this rule of using Upwork instead of Fiverr for specialized talent. Take, for example, a recent search I conducted for a child voice actor to narrate a children's audiobook. Despite posting on Upwork, the responses didn't bring forth the right candidates. This led me to explore Voices.com, a platform known for its niche focus on talented and accredited voice actors. Although I encountered a number of accredited child voice actors on Voices.com, their fees were beyond my allocated budget. Turning to Fiverr.com, I was fortunate to discover a gifted child voice actor who met my quality expectations and budgetary constraints.

My inclination towards Upwork extends beyond talent discovery. Their customer service is notably superior, offering live chat support that aligns with standard U.S. business hours facilitating real-time assistance when needed. Fiverr's support system, on the other hand, operates through a help desk, which, in my personal experience, has sometimes failed to respond to inquiries. This level of accessibility and reliability in customer service is why Upwork is often my first choice for freelance collaborations.

Although both Fiverr and Upwork have their merits, if you're looking for a platform that aligns with professional, long-term projects, Upwork is a clear choice. Among the two reasons I listed above, here are some additional reasons.

Depth of Talent Pool

Upwork boasts a diverse and extensive pool of freelancers, from graphic designers to software developers. Unlike Fiverr, which is often associated with one-off gigs, Upwork is the go-to for businesses seeking professionals for comprehensive projects. The platform's rigorous vetting process ensures that you're engaging with highly skilled individuals committed to delivering quality work.

Flexible Hiring Models

Upwork offers a more flexible hiring model compared to Fiverr. You can post a job and receive bids or search for freelancers and view detailed profiles before initiating contact. This allows for a tailored approach to hiring, ensuring you find the perfect match for your project's specific needs.

Project Management Tools

Upwork's platform is designed with project management in mind. It provides a suite of tools that facilitate communication, time tracking, and milestone payments, which are essential for larger projects. These features provide transparency and foster trust between you and your freelancer, something that's less structured on Fiverr.

Quality Assurance

Upwork's feedback system is comprehensive, providing insights into a freelancer's past performance on similar projects. This, combined with Upwork's Payment Protection, ensures that you pay for work that meets your standards. While Fiverr also has a rating system, the emphasis on quick, lower-cost gigs can sometimes mean quality takes a backseat.

Conclusion

For businesses seeking a professional, reliable, and quality-driven experience, Upwork stands out. It's not just about getting the job done; it's about building relationships with top-tier freelancers who can bring value to your projects time and time again. Choose Upwork for a partnership that grows with your business.

However, if you find the need to use Fiverr instead of Upwork or another platform, here's a guide to hiring freelancers on Fiverr:

1. Define Your Project Needs

Before diving into the sea of Fiverr gigs, take a moment to clearly define what you need. A well-articulated project brief not only helps you find the right talent but also ensures the freelancer can deliver exactly what you're looking for. Be specific about your project's scope, deadlines, and any must-haves or deal-breakers.

2. Search and Select

Fiverr's search function is robust. Use keywords related to your project to find gigs offering the services you need. Don't rush this step. Take your time to browse through the results, paying close attention to gig descriptions, portfolios, and customer reviews.

3. Evaluate Seller Levels and Reviews

Fiverr categorizes sellers based on their level of service and experience, from New Sellers to Top-Rated Sellers. While higher levels often indicate more experience and higher customer satisfaction, don't overlook newcomers. They can be hidden gems with the right expertise at competitive prices. Reviews are telling; they reflect real experiences from past clients. Look for comments that speak to the seller's professionalism, communication, and quality of work.

4. Communicate before You Commit

Once you've shortlisted a few potential freelancers, reach out to them. Fiverr's messaging system allows you to discuss your project and clarify any questions. This step is crucial for gauging responsiveness and getting a feel for their communication style.

5. Start Small

If you're working with a freelancer for the first time, consider a trial run with a smaller aspect of your project. This minimizes risk and gives you a firsthand look at their work ethic and deliverable quality.

6. Place Your Order

When you're ready, go ahead and place your order. Be sure to provide all necessary information and files to help the freelancer get started. Clear and concise instructions can make the difference between a good outcome and a great one.

7. Review and Revise

Once the freelancer delivers the work, review it thoroughly. If revisions are needed, provide constructive feedback. Remember, clear communication is key to getting the results you want.

8. Finalize and Follow-up

If you're satisfied with the work, complete the order and leave an honest review. Building a relationship with a freelancer can lead to a reliable partnership for future projects.

9. Manage Your Orders

Keep track of your ongoing and completed orders. Fiverr's

dashboard is designed to help you manage your projects efficiently, so take advantage of it.

10. Scale Up

As you become more familiar with Fiverr and establish relationships with freelancers, you can scale up your projects. With confidence in your freelancers' abilities, you can entrust them with larger, more complex tasks.

By following these steps, you'll be well on your way to harnessing the full potential of Fiverr to meet your business needs. Remember, every successful project on Fiverr starts with clear communication and ends with a review that helps the entire community thrive. Happy hiring!

Chapter 17: Evaluating Freelancers Prior to Hiring

In this segment, I'll be sharing insights on selecting top-notch freelancers and assessing their capabilities. Generally, you have two routes: engaging an individual freelancer or contracting with an agency. While both have their merits, I tend to favor individual freelancers. The direct line of communication with the person handling your tasks is invaluable. With agencies, the risk of your instructions getting lost in translation through a chain of command is higher, and often, you might find your work in the hands of someone you've never directly interacted with.

When you partner with an individual, their portfolio is a transparent window into their capabilities, showcasing their achievements and the quality of work you can expect. With agencies, it's trickier to pinpoint who exactly contributed to a piece of work and to what extent. Upwork conveniently indicates if a freelancer is associated with an agency right in their proposal, which is a detail I appreciate for making informed decisions. Another aspect to weigh is the freelancer's country of origin relative to the nature of the job.

Now, I say this with the utmost respect and based on extensive experience: for writing tasks, I prioritize freelancers from countries where English is the native language. The nuance and depth of understanding that native speakers bring to the table are typically unmatched. While you may encounter non-native English speakers offering competitive rates, the adage "you get what you pay for" often rings true. I've worked with individuals from various non-English speaking regions for writing projects, and the results have consistently confirmed my approach. Choosing a native English speaker has invariably led to superior outcomes for writing jobs.

This rule applies to all writing jobs: Regardless of the language, always hire native speakers to write. On numerous occasions, I have hired native Spanish speakers for Spanish-language writing jobs. On one occasion, I broke my own rule and hired a non-native Spanish speaker to do a Spanish-language writing job. In that instance, I hired an American woman who taught Spanish for many years in the U.S. public school system. When she completed the job, I quickly realized that the quality of her work was not on par with the writing jobs that I paid to be performed by native Spanish speakers from Latin American countries.

Navigating the world of virtual assistance, I've found the Philippines to be an exceptional source. Their work ethic there is commendable, and their proficiency in English—both spoken and written—is impressive, making them ideal for a variety of tasks. However, when it comes to software and app development, my experiences have led me to favor the technical prowess of Eastern European developers. They seem to have a robust culture of development. That said, I've also encountered highly skilled developers and programmers from Argentina and India.

In the realm of graphic design, Eastern Europe and the Philippines often yield talented individuals. Yet, it's worth noting that I've discovered equally talented designers from India, Turkey, Egypt, and Venezuela through Upwork. It's important to mention that professionals from English-speaking countries tend to command higher rates for graphic design and development work, which is why looking outside of English-speaking countries can be more cost-effective without compromising on quality.

Language is a critical factor in graphic and design work. Clear communication is non-negotiable to avoid unnecessary complications and frustrations. When reviewing proposals, the applicant's language skills should give you a clear indication of their ability to collaborate effectively. Trust your instincts here. While it might be tempting to opt for a less expensive option, I've learned that this often leads to more trouble than it's worth.

For optimal results, focus on specialists rather than generalists. A jack-of-all-trades might be a valuable virtual assistant, but they may not excel in the specific task you need. Always aim to hire someone with a proven track record in the specific field you require. And here's a crucial tip: don't commit to a significant project with someone new. Start with smaller tasks and build up as they prove their reliability and skill. Platforms like Upwork make it easy to review a freelancer's history, earnings, and feedback from previous jobs. A solid portfolio is a must, and if a freelancer can't provide one, it's wise to consider other candidates. Upwork profiles are a treasure trove of such information, allowing you to make informed hiring decisions.

When you're diving into the hiring process online, the ability to scrutinize past feedback on a freelancer's profile is invaluable. It's a transparent window into their professional history, simplifying the vetting process considerably. Modern platforms have streamlined this even further. Take 99designs, for instance, where you can rate designs with a star system, or Upwork, which offers a straightforward thumbs up or thumbs down approach. This feature is particularly handy when you're inundated with proposals and need to swiftly sort through them.

For example, if you're seeking a seasoned professional and stumble upon a profile that shows only $40 earned on Upwork, a thumbs down can help you move on without a second thought. Similarly, if you're in need of a native Spanish speaker for translation work and receive applications from regions that don't fit the bill, a quick thumbs down helps you filter out the mismatched candidates. This way, you can whittle down a daunting list of 50 to a manageable five or six prime candidates in no time.

As you progress, you'll only engage with those you've marked positively, saving precious time. The goal is to swiftly pinpoint the most promising candidates and then invest more time in those select few as you move through the hiring stages. My experience on Upwork has shown that you can often quickly eliminate a swath of applicants by assessing their experience, geographical location, and the effort they put into their cover letters. Then, as you draw closer to making a hire, you delve deeper, much like the multi-stage interview process in the traditional job market. If you've ever been on either side of that process, you'll recognize the increasing specificity and detail required as you progress—principles that are just as applicable to online hiring.

Chapter 18: Navigating Potential Hiring Pitfalls

In this chapter, we explore various red flags and cautionary indicators that might arise in your journey of hiring or collaborating with freelancers. A notable concern is freelancers requesting upfront payment. This scenario is familiar to us: Upon funding an initial project milestone, a freelancer might request its release before commencing work. In platforms like Upwork, where you might often set multiple milestones for a project, it's imperative to be vigilant if a freelancer insists on prematurely releasing funds.

The importance of safeguarding these funds cannot be overstated, as once released, they are held securely by the platform until that point. This necessitates caution when a newly hired freelancer seeks early payment without any work progress. Although exceptions exist, such as established trust or direct engagements outside platforms, the default stance should generally favor post-completion payments. This approach not only secures your investment but also aligns with the protective mechanisms offered by platforms, thereby safeguarding your business's best interests.

So, when engaging with a new freelancer, it's wise to withhold upfront payments unless a specific, compelling justification is present. This practice serves as a protective measure against potential fraudulent activities. On platforms like Upwork, should any concerning behavior surface, you have the option to report the freelancer. Freelancers typically avoid such disputes due to the adverse impact on their reputation and future opportunities.

Be particularly cautious with unexpected cost escalations, especially from new freelancers. While seasoned professionals may have legitimate reasons for price adjustments, it's not uncommon for less experienced freelancers to use this as a leverage tactic against clients new to the platform. To avoid being taken advantage of, scrutinize such requests carefully and hold your ground if necessary.

The significance of clear and detailed job descriptions in managing expectations cannot be overstated. My extensive experience of over two decades in hiring freelancers, starting with Elance (now Upwork), has reinforced the value of explicit communication right from the start of a project. Platforms like Upwork, having matured over the years, offer robust review and feedback systems that significantly benefit clients. Most complications tend to arise either from ambiguities in job requirements or from receiving work of inferior quality. By thoroughly vetting applicants and strategically using platform features such as milestone settings, you can effectively shield yourself from these common pitfalls.

In summary, understanding and recognizing these red flags can immensely aid in fostering successful and secure freelance engagements. Awareness and appropriate use of platform features, coupled with clear communication and contractual terms, can help navigate and mitigate potential risks in the freelance hiring process.

Chapter 19: Effectively Communicating Post-hire Instructions

Let's take a deeper look into the process of establishing effective post-hire instructions. Our focus here centers around crafting detailed job guidelines for individuals once they have formally accepted a position. Imagine using a platform like Upwork as a baseline. Initially, we present a succinct job description, capturing the essence of the role. This is just a preliminary step. The real crux comes after hiring, where we provide our new hires with far more elaborate instructions. This method is deliberately straightforward and transparent, making it easy for anyone to grasp the requirements of the job. It also offers an essential exit route for hires who, upon delving into these detailed instructions, may find the role unsuitable or lose interest. Although such occurrences are relatively rare in my experience, they are more frequent with newcomers to the platform.

This methodology acts as a protective measure. In the event of a dispute regarding the quality of work, these comprehensive instructions become a crucial reference point. They serve to illustrate the gap between the expected deliverables and what was actually produced. The beauty of using a platform like Upwork lies in its ability to document every interaction and instruction, creating a verifiable paper trail. Should a discrepancy arise, you can effortlessly point to the specific requirements you had outlined which were not met in the final output.

While I must emphasize that disputes are quite uncommon, it's undeniable that our meticulous approach to this process significantly mitigates such risks. This detailed explanation underscores the importance of this approach, ensuring that you are not only prepared but also positioned advantageously to secure the most favorable results in your engagements.

In the realm of post-hire communications, dedicating time to meticulously detail the task at hand is not just beneficial; it's essential. The intricacy of the job often dictates the communication mode. Options range from utilizing the platform's built-in chat or messaging features to more direct methods like Zoom, Skype, or WhatsApp calls. For particularly complex or nuanced tasks, leveraging video tools such as Loom, which offers an intuitive screen-sharing service, can be exceptionally effective.

The choice of communication method should be thoughtfully considered, as each offers unique benefits and potential limitations. The level of detail in your instructions should be proportionate to the job's complexity. Simpler tasks might require just a brief overview, while more intricate or time-saving tasks warrant thorough, detailed explanations. The key is to avoid presuming the freelancer understands your expectations implicitly. It's your responsibility to ensure every aspect of the task is communicated explicitly and understood.

In my experience, Loom has been an invaluable tool for conveying precise requirements to freelancers. This method has proven to be more efficient and effective than merely sending static screenshots. For those unfamiliar with Loom, it is a user-friendly screen recorder that's compatible with various operating systems, including Mac and Windows. Also, it supports mobile platforms like iOS and Android. Its ease of installation and use, coupled with the fact that it's free, makes it a preferable option for many. While similar in function to TechSmith's Camtasia, a notable distinction is that Loom offers its services without charge, unlike Camtasia.

The objective in creating these instructional videos is NOT to achieve a polished, professional finish; the focus should be on clarity and comprehensiveness. Video explanations can often convey nuances and details more effectively than written text or audio calls. They offer a visual representation that can be crucial for complex tasks. However, whichever method you opt for, it's imperative to commit to developing clear, thorough instructions. This clarity not only sets the stage for a successful collaboration but also ensures that your expectations are fully understood by the freelancer. This approach not only facilitates effective work completion but also fosters a professional and mutually respectful working relationship.

Chapter 20: Putting Your Freelancers to the Final Test

When it comes to successfully hiring freelancers, especially for substantial projects, there's a strategy I've found particularly effective. This approach is not solely focused on the quality of the work but also aims to understand the dynamics of working with the freelancer. Suppose you're planning to hire someone from Upwork for a significant project, like creating 30 blog posts.

In such cases, breaking the task into smaller, manageable milestones is a smart move. For instance, you could begin with a batch of 5 blog posts, then increase to 10 for the next phase, and finally, complete the set with 15 more. This phased method allows you to assess the quality of the work right from the start, provide constructive feedback, and make an informed decision on whether to continue with the same freelancer or look for another.

One major advantage of platforms like Upwork is their inherent flexibility. If the initial phase doesn't meet your expectations, your commitment is limited only to that part of the work. This significantly reduces your financial risk and exposure. Another effective tactic is to start with a very small task. For instance, before committing to a large order of 30 blog posts, you might assign a trial task of just two posts. This preliminary step offers a glimpse into the freelancer's work and sets the stage for potential ongoing work.

I always advocate for transparency in these dealings. There's no need for vague or indirect methods. Be upfront with freelancers about the fact that the initial task is a test to see if their work aligns with your standards and if the two of you can collaborate effectively on larger projects. This honesty sets clear expectations and fosters a relationship of mutual understanding and respect.

Moreover, this testing phase can reveal much more than just the quality of work. It can demonstrate a freelancer's reliability, responsiveness to feedback, ability to meet deadlines, and adaptability to your business's tone and style. These factors are crucial in determining whether a freelancer is suitable for long-term collaboration.

In essence, trialing a freelancer with a small task or milestone is an integral step not just in gauging their capability but in laying the groundwork for what could turn out to be a long-term, productive outsourcing partnership. It's about ensuring you invest your resources in someone who is not just technically skilled but also meshes well with your business's culture and operational style. This strategy has been a key component in my success with outsourcing, ensuring that I build a team that is not only talented but also aligned with my business's vision and work ethic.

Chapter 21: A Bird's Eye View of Freelancer Management

Managing freelancers involves more than just delegating tasks; it's about building a relationship based on clear communication and mutual respect. Establishing clear duties and responsibilities from the outset is not just a matter of organizational efficiency; it also sets the tone for the quality of work you expect. This clarity is achieved not only through what you communicate but also by how you ensure the freelancer has a complete understanding of the tasks at hand. Regular check-ins and clarifications can go a long way in ensuring that both parties are on the same page.

Providing positive and constructive feedback is another cornerstone of effective freelancer management. When working with freelancers, such as article writers, the goal often extends beyond a single project. You are likely to collaborate with them repeatedly, making it crucial to establish a rapport where constructive criticism is welcomed and understood as a means to enhance future work. When offering feedback, it's beneficial to frame it in a way that highlights its purpose: to refine and improve work for future tasks. This approach not only helps maintain a positive working environment but also encourages a growth mindset.

Furthermore, when initial work does not meet expectations, it's essential to balance critiques with recognition of what has been done well. This approach helps in maintaining a freelancer's motivation and confidence. Communication nuances become even more significant in remote and digital interactions. Emails and chats, which are often the primary modes of communication with freelancers, can easily misrepresent the intended tone, especially when dealing with other cultures. What may be intended as a succinct, efficient response can unintentionally come across as brusque or dismissive. Being aware of these potential misunderstandings and taking the time to craft messages thoughtfully can prevent miscommunication and foster a more productive and harmonious working relationship.

Managing freelancers effectively is a blend of clear communication, thoughtful feedback, and cultural sensitivity. It's about creating a professional environment where expectations are well-defined, feedback is used constructively, and communication is tailored to avoid misinterpretations. This approach not only ensures the quality of work but also builds a foundation for ongoing, successful collaborations.

Being cautious about how your communications are perceived is crucial in maintaining a positive and productive working relationship with your freelancers. Starting with positive feedback is a strategy that sets a constructive tone, especially when there are areas of improvement to be addressed. This approach helps avoid putting the relationship into a negative space, something that's essential to sidestep. While being courteous and polite is necessary, it's equally important to maintain a balance and not venture into over-familiarity. Keeping interactions professional ensures that when the time comes to discuss changes or provide feedback, it's received in the right spirit, free from personal biases or misunderstandings.

The importance of steering clear of micromanagement cannot be overstated in the context of outsourcing. The essence of delegating tasks is to entrust responsibilities and not to oversee every minor detail. We've observed that allowing freelancers to take ownership and lead their tasks results in the most productive outcomes. Frequent check-ins and micromanaging not only drain your time but also hinder the freelancer's ability to work effectively and independently. It's a practice that contradicts the primary objective of outsourcing, which is to streamline processes and free up your time.

Moreover, micromanagement can lead to a strained working environment, often resulting in frustration and diminished morale for the freelancer. This underlines the importance of a careful and thoughtful selection of freelancers. Choosing the right individual for the task is a critical step that can prevent the need for excessive oversight. If you find yourself in a position where micromanagement becomes a necessity, it's a strong indicator that the freelancer may not be the right fit for the job. In such cases, reassessing your choice and finding someone more aligned with your work style and requirements might be the best course of action. Ultimately, successful outsourcing is about building trust and empowering your team to deliver results independently, fostering an environment where both parties can thrive.

The key to preventing micromanagement lies in crafting crystal-clear instructions from the outset. Taking this extra time in the beginning to detail the project's requirements can significantly reduce the need for ongoing adjustments. This approach not only conserves your time but also empowers the freelancer to work more autonomously and confidently. The frequency of your check-ins with the freelancer should align with the project's timeline and complexity. For example, in a lengthy project like a 35-hour audio translation, periodic updates every few days might suffice. This approach balances oversight with autonomy, allowing the freelancer space to progress while keeping you informed.

On the other hand, for shorter, more time-sensitive projects, more frequent communication may be necessary to ensure the project is on track. Prompt feedback in these scenarios can prevent last-minute surprises and ensure the final product aligns with your expectations. However, it's crucial to balance this need for information with the freelancer's need for uninterrupted work time.

When collaborating with specialists like designers, it's important to recognize and respect their expertise. While you may have a vision for your project, like a specific logo design, it's beneficial to remain open to the designer's creative input. They bring a professional eye for aesthetics that can enhance your ideas. Trusting their judgment and allowing them some creative freedom can lead to more innovative and effective design outcomes.

In certain types of work, particularly creative tasks like writing, reviewing incomplete drafts may not always provide an accurate representation of the final quality. For instance, assessing an article before it has undergone proofreading and editing can lead to unnecessary concerns about errors that would typically be resolved in the final stages. In contrast, for projects where your expertise and insight are crucial, like ghostwriting a book on a topic you're passionate about, regular check-ins can be instrumental in ensuring the content aligns with your vision and standards. Deciding when and how often to review progress depends on the nature of the task and your involvement level. Striking the right balance between giving guidance and allowing independence is key to successful freelancer management. This balance fosters a productive working environment where both you and the freelancer can achieve your best work.

Chapter 22: Effective Management Tools

Management tools are pivotal in orchestrating complex projects, especially when dealing with a globally distributed team. Their ability to provide a 'big picture' perspective is invaluable in ensuring all parts of the project are moving in harmony. When team members are spread across diverse time zones, from Eastern Europe to India to the UK and the USA, these tools bridge the gap, enabling real-time collaboration and communication. This global reach ensures that everyone, regardless of their location, is seamlessly integrated into the workflow.

In addition to facilitating communication, these tools excel in task allocation and progress tracking. They allow managers to assign tasks to team members, set deadlines, and monitor progress, all within a unified platform. This visibility into each team member's contributions and deadlines helps preempt bottlenecks and keep the project on track.

Trello:

Trello, as an example, exemplifies these benefits. Its board-and-card system makes it easy to organize tasks, while its visual interface is user-friendly and effective in portraying the status of various tasks. Trello's adaptability to different project types makes it a versatile choice, whether you're managing a software development project, a marketing campaign, or any other collaborative effort.

In my own experience with a mobile app development project, these tools have been indispensable. They have enabled us to coordinate between developers in India and a QA professional in Venezuela, ensuring that the app is developed and tested efficiently.

Meanwhile, our team member in Argentina, with his expertise in app development and marketing, uses the same platform to manage the app submission to the app stores. This cohesive use of management tools creates a streamlined process where everyone is aware of their roles, responsibilities, and the overall progress of the project.

Effective use of management tools like Trello can revolutionize how projects are managed, especially in a landscape where teams are often geographically and culturally diverse. These tools not only enhance communication and collaboration but also provide the necessary structure and oversight to ensure project success. They are essential for any project manager or team leader looking to optimize their team's efficiency and productivity in a globalized work environment.

Trello stands out as an exceptional tool and even offers a free version. Trello's pricing structure includes four tiers: Free, Standard, Premium, and Enterprise. The free tier is ideal for individuals or small teams, providing essential functionalities to manage tasks effectively. For those new to Trello, the free plan usually suffices. We chose Trello because our development team was already familiar with it. When a team member is already proficient with a management tool, it often makes sense for the entire team to adopt the same tool for consistency and convenience.

One aspect of Trello I particularly appreciate is its ability to organize tasks into lists while offering an overarching view of the entire day's workload. This feature makes it an excellent tool for planning and prioritizing tasks. Trello's functionality allows for the creation of a 'Daily Tasks' list, which can be transferred into a 'To Do Today' list each day. Moreover, if a task in the 'Backlog' is due tomorrow, it automatically shifts to the 'To Do Today' list.

The visual nature of Trello is another significant advantage. It provides a quick snapshot of ongoing activities. However, the true gem of Trello is its board, which is the core of the application. The Trello board operates on the Kanban principles, a methodology originating in Japan for efficient inventory management and later adapted for project management.

Trello also helps us track various stages of a project: tasks that are complete but awaiting feedback, those that are on hold, and a verification list. The versatility in setting up Trello boards makes it an effective tool for managing different projects. It's simplicity personified, avoiding unnecessary complications. With Trello, we gain a bird's eye view of ongoing tasks and the overall project status, enhancing our project management efficiency.

One advantage of a platform such as Trello and several of the other platforms I'll mention in this section is that you have the option to start with a free plan and then upgrade as your business grows and your needs evolve. There's no necessity to commence with the most expensive plans offered by these platforms. Starting small and scaling up as needed can be a more practical and cost-effective approach.

Basecamp:
Basecamp is another management and collaboration tool we've found to be extremely efficient. In several of our businesses, we use Basecamp every day. The aspect of Basecamp I appreciate most is its ability to centralize communication effectively.

At the time I'm writing this, Basecamp's most affordable plan appears to be around $15 per month per user. Notably, Basecamp charges only for employees, while guests can be added at no extra cost. For businesses experiencing rapid growth, with various components and team members in different locations, Basecamp proves to be an invaluable resource.

In our publishing business, for instance, we handle all our communications through Basecamp. This includes interactions among team members and conversations with ghostwriters, editors, and proofreaders. Adding new members to Basecamp is a straightforward process.

One of the key advantages of Basecamp, which is true for other management tools as well, is the ability to create a comprehensive paper trail. If a team member departs or transitions to a different role, we have a complete record of past communications and activities. This transparency is incredibly beneficial when introducing someone new to an existing role or restructuring the personnel in your organization. In essence, Basecamp is an exceptionally useful tool for managing team dynamics and workflow.

Hubstaff:

Hubstaff is another tool that we find invaluable in our operations. It's an employee work tracker that offers features like screenshots, timesheets, billing, and comprehensive reports. Essentially, Hubstaff is a time-tracking and workforce management platform designed to streamline the management of a growing business.

We primarily use Hubstaff when coordinating a large number of team members and contractors who are working on different tasks at various times. Hubstaff enables us to monitor ongoing activities effectively. It allows team members to easily log their hours, providing transparency about the time spent on tasks – whether it's 4.5 hours today or 7.5 hours yesterday. Workers can manually input and adjust their time logs, which the system then integrates seamlessly.

A notable feature of Hubstaff is its ability to take screenshots of team members' computers, offering flexibility in its setup. While some might be hesitant about this aspect, we've made it part of our company policy. We have made it clear that using Hubstaff isn't primarily about supervising workers; rather, it's more focused on accurately recording time to streamline project management and accounting processes. This feature also serves as a safeguard, particularly when working with new contractors, ensuring that reported work hours are accurate and preventing any discrepancies.

This way, we can maintain fairness and transparency in our billing and project management.

To sum it all up, when considering any management platform, you must consider the value of the platform in relation to its cost. Ask yourself, "Is this platform or tool worth the investment? Will it contribute to my business's growth?" Ideally, your answer should be affirmative to both of these questions. The tools I've mentioned in this section allow for the smooth integration of new team members to undertake various roles. Many of these tools are designed to scale with your business, with pricing that adjusts as your company expands.

Chapter 23: Effectively Resolving Issues with Freelancers

Today, let's discuss resolving issues with freelancers and some effective strategies we've found. A common challenge when working with freelancers, particularly new ones, is receiving work that doesn't meet your standards. This can happen even if their past work samples seemed promising. The benefit of using outsourcing platforms like Upwork or 99 Designs is their payment model: you pay only when you're satisfied with the work. If the work doesn't meet your expectations, you can ask the freelancer to revise it. With Upwork, should you conclude that the freelancer is unable to deliver satisfactory work, you have the option to end the contract and request a refund for any funded milestone. The freelancer can then approve this refund, and the money you've funded will be returned to you, allowing you to find another freelancer and establish a new milestone.

However, it's important to remember that requesting a refund doesn't guarantee the freelancer will agree to it. If a freelancer declines your refund request, the issue moves to a formal dispute and enters mediation. During mediation, an Upwork mediator works to facilitate a mutual agreement between you and the freelancer regarding the payment. If an agreement can't be reached, there is the option to proceed to arbitration. Mediation doesn't automatically imply that Upwork will rule in the client's favor; it's more about attempting to find a fair resolution for both parties. In reality, platforms such as Upwork, Fiverr, and 99 Designs have two clients. One is the business owner (you), and the other is the freelancer. Their platforms require both parties for them to function successfully.

It's important to remember that on Upwork, payments are often structured around pre-set milestones. If you've set up a small initial milestone to assess the quality of a freelancer's work, you might consider releasing the funds even if the freelancer doesn't agree to a refund. Typically, a freelancer will agree to refund a small amount if the work isn't up to par, as they would likely prefer to avoid a negative review. Given that the amount in question is small, it's generally not worth it for the freelancer to risk a negative review on their profile over a modest sum of money.

However, as a business owner, you bear the responsibility of ensuring that you've clearly and thoroughly communicated everything about the job and your expectations right from the start. Miscommunications can occur, often stemming from differing ideas or expectations between you and the freelancer. It's essential to ensure that both parties are on the same page. In case of any issues with the quality of the work, it's helpful to refer back to your initial project description. For example, you can point out specific aspects that were crucial, saying something like, "One of the key requirements was this particular element." This approach helps clarify any misunderstandings and realign the project's objectives.

Using examples can be incredibly effective, particularly in graphics-related projects, to ensure everyone understands the project requirements. Clarifying why certain tasks need to be done a certain way can facilitate the freelancer's ability to meet your expectations. However, if issues with the quality of work persist despite thorough explanations and the freelancer is still unable to deliver what you need, it may be necessary to find someone else before setting any new milestones. Often, it becomes apparent quite early whether a freelancer possesses the required skills and motivation. If they don't seem capable or willing to meet your expectations, it's not advisable to linger in the hope that their work will improve. Instead, consider requesting a refund or releasing the initially funded small milestone amount and seek another freelancer who is better suited for the job.

Remember, the objective is not to spend excessive time training someone to fit your ideal freelancer profile. Ideally, the freelancer you choose should already possess the necessary skills and motivation to perform the job effectively. Your goal isn't to train someone on the job but to find a competent and motivated individual who can deliver the goods.

In my experience, issues with low-quality work often arise from a lack of necessary skills. Besides low-quality work, another common issue is missed deadlines. A strategy I employ is to set a deadline a few days earlier than when I actually need the work. For instance, if I need something by Friday the 13th, I might set the deadline for Monday the 9th. This buffer allows for unforeseen circumstances. It's important to remember that freelancers, like anyone, can face personal challenges or external factors beyond their control. For example, there are parts of the world where natural disasters are more frequent than in the U.S., and the effects are commonly more devastating. And such effects can also greatly impact a freelancer's ability to work. Being aware of these potentialities and offering a degree of empathy and flexibility, at least initially, can be beneficial in maintaining a healthy working relationship.

On the other hand, consistently missing deadlines can significantly hinder a business's growth, so it's crucial to address this issue. Occasional lapses might be understandable, and in such cases, I tend to give the freelancer the benefit of the doubt. However, regular missed deadlines are unacceptable and a valid reason to consider hiring someone else.

Another issue is that freelancers sometimes underestimate the scope of a project or the time it will take, which can be challenging to predict. However, experienced freelancers should be able to estimate and meet deadlines accurately. Occasionally, you might encounter freelancers who lack the necessary skills or find that a project takes longer than they expected. There are even rare instances where a freelancer might act as a middleman, outsourcing your project to someone else unbeknownst to you, which is certainly not desirable.

Another issue arises when freelancers bid too low for a job, leading to a lack of motivation to complete the work properly. For example, they might quote $100 for a task that realistically should be priced at $200 or more. This can result in slow or substandard work. Sometimes, a freelancer might be juggling too many jobs simultaneously, affecting their focus on your project. It's clear that such situations are not your responsibility, but they do happen. While I prefer to start by giving freelancers the benefit of the doubt, consistent failure to meet deadlines or expectations means it's time to find a new freelancer.

Before ending the relationship with a freelancer, it's critical to change any passwords to tools or services they had access to. This precaution prevents any potential retaliatory actions that could harm your business. Although such incidents are rare, and you can report any malicious behavior to platforms like Upwork, it's better to be safe than sorry. Most freelancers, particularly in developing countries, value their platform presence highly due to limited job opportunities, so they are unlikely to risk being banned. However, ensuring that all access is revoked before terminating the contract is a prudent step to safeguard your business interests.

Chapter 24: Harmonizing Outsourced & In-House Teams for Business Success

In the realm of small businesses, the integration of outsourced teams with in-house staff is a strategic move toward growth and scalability. This chapter delves into effective methods for seamlessly blending these two facets of your workforce, ensuring they work together to achieve your business objectives.

Cultivating Effective Communication

Effective communication forms the bedrock of a successful integration between outsourced and in-house teams. It's imperative to establish robust communication channels and protocols. Utilizing collaborative tools such as Asana, Trello, Basecamp, or Slack can streamline interactions, ensuring all team members, regardless of their location, stay connected and informed. Regular video calls and virtual meetings can also serve as tools for maintaining a sense of team unity and ensuring clarity in project goals and expectations.

Embracing Cultural Diversity

Outsourced teams often bring diverse cultural backgrounds, enriching your business with a variety of perspectives. Embracing this diversity requires a commitment to cultural sensitivity and inclusion. Foster an environment where cultural differences are not just tolerated but celebrated. Initiatives like cross-cultural training sessions, sharing cultural practices, and acknowledging international holidays can greatly enhance mutual understanding and respect.

Clear Definition of Roles and Responsibilities

Ambiguity in roles and responsibilities can lead to inefficiencies and friction between teams. It's crucial to delineate clear roles for each team member, ensuring everyone understands their specific duties and how their work contributes to the broader goals of the project or organization. Regularly revisiting and adjusting these roles can help keep the teams aligned and focused.

Fostering Trust and Team Cohesion

Developing trust between outsourced and in-house teams is essential for a harmonious working relationship. This trust is fostered through transparency in operations and open, honest communication. Engage in team-building activities that can be conducted remotely, such as virtual coffee breaks or team challenges, to build camaraderie and a sense of belonging among team members.

Streamlining Performance Management

An integrated performance management approach for outsourced and in-house teams is crucial. Set up measurable performance indicators and regular review sessions to assess progress. Providing consistent and constructive feedback helps identify areas for improvement and acknowledge achievements, which motivates team members and drives productivity.

Aligning with Organizational Goals

The importance of alignment of both in-house and outsourced teams with your business's overall objectives cannot be overstated.

Regular briefings on the company's vision, updates on progress, and discussions on long-term goals ensure that every team member is working towards the same end. This shared vision not only enhances productivity but also fosters a deeper connection with the company's mission.

Conflict Resolution Strategies

Differences in opinion and working styles can lead to conflicts. Establishing effective conflict resolution mechanisms is vital. This might involve setting up a mediation process or having a structured approach to problem-solving. Addressing conflicts quickly and constructively is key to maintaining a positive work environment and preventing any negative impact on team morale.

Legal and Ethical Compliance

Integrating outsourced teams requires adherence to various legal and ethical standards, including labor laws, data protection regulations, and confidentiality agreements. Ensuring that these legalities are understood and respected by all team members is essential in building a secure and compliant working environment.

Continuous Improvement and Adaptation

The business landscape is constantly evolving, and so should your approach to team integration. Regular feedback sessions with in-house and outsourced team members can provide valuable insights into the effectiveness of your integration strategies. Be prepared to adapt and refine these strategies to meet the changing needs of your business and workforce.

Conclusion

The integration of outsourced teams with in-house staff, when executed effectively, can lead to a dynamic, innovative, and productive workforce. By prioritizing clear communication, embracing cultural diversity, defining roles, building trust, managing performance, aligning goals, resolving conflicts, and ensuring legal compliance, your business can harness the full potential of a diverse and collaborative team. This approach not only drives operational efficiency but also creates a work culture that values unity and cooperation, propelling your business toward new heights of success.

Chapter 25: The Art of Scaling Your Outsourcing

Scaling is a critical aspect of business growth, and it involves more than just increasing your workforce; it's about strategic expansion. As your business scales up, the need to hire more people becomes evident. However, this expansion should align with the growth of your business to avoid overburdening your financial resources. Rapid hiring might seem like a quick solution to growth challenges, but it can lead to disproportionate overhead costs, potentially impacting your profitability.

The key is to scale responsibly and methodically. This means closely monitoring the correlation between your revenue growth and team expansion. Each new hire should ideally contribute to either directly increasing your revenue or significantly improving operational efficiency, which, in turn, indirectly affects your bottom line. For instance, a marketing manager can directly influence revenue through effective marketing strategies, while a CFO can streamline your financial operations, identifying cost-saving opportunities and enhancing profitability.

In certain scenarios, the impact of a new hire on your bottom line may not be immediately apparent but is nonetheless crucial. Roles focused on customer service, for instance, may not directly increase revenue but play a vital role in customer retention and satisfaction, which are key to long-term business success. Similarly, IT or HR roles contribute to the smooth running of your business operations, which, while not directly impacting revenue, are essential for sustainable growth.

As you scale, it's also important to consider the balance between in-house hires and outsourced talent. Outsourcing can often provide a more flexible and cost-effective solution for certain functions, especially when you're in the process of scaling. It allows you to access specialized skills and services as needed without the commitment of full-time salaries and benefits. So scaling your team as your business grows is a delicate balancing act. It requires careful planning, a clear understanding of your business needs, and a strategic approach to hiring. By aligning team growth with income growth and ensuring each new hire contributes to your business's success, you can scale effectively and sustainably.

Having a vivid and well-defined vision for your business is more than just setting goals; it's about understanding the intricate workings of your business and how each element contributes to the bigger picture. Just like a machine with various components, each team member or business process plays a specific and crucial role. It's vital to ensure that every component, or in this case, every person and process, is necessary and contributes to the efficiency of the business. Redundant or non-essential elements can be resource-draining, and identifying these early can prevent unnecessary expenditure and complexity.

Mapping out your business plan is a practical step in bringing this vision to life. This visual representation helps in identifying the key functions, roles, and resources required. It allows you to break down your ultimate goal into actionable steps and understand the resources needed at each stage.

When it comes to assembling your team, the focus should be on aligning skills and roles with the needs of your business. Each team member should be like a cog in the machine, essential to its smooth operation. Ask yourself: What roles are critical for operational efficiency? What skills and attributes will these roles require? This clarity in your team's composition ensures that each member is not just filling a position but actively contributing to the business's growth and success.

Moreover, understanding the skills and attributes needed for each role enables you to make informed hiring decisions. This insight is invaluable when it comes to selecting the right individuals who not only have the necessary skills but also fit into the culture and vision of your company. Visualizing your business as a well-oiled machine, with each component playing a vital role, can guide you in structuring your team and resources effectively. This approach ensures that every aspect of your business is aligned with your overarching vision, setting a solid foundation for growth and success.

Scaling your team in tandem with revenue growth is a delicate yet essential process. As I mentioned earlier, the decision to scale should be timed with increasing revenue because as your business grows, the demands and complexities of operations also expand. If you don't scale your team accordingly, you may find yourself overwhelmed with additional tasks or, worse, see your business's growth plateau or decline.

As the CEO or business leader, your role is to maintain a strategic overview, guiding the direction of your business. You're the orchestrator of your business's growth, pulling different levers to achieve the best outcomes. By strategically hiring new team members, you can stay focused on high-level decisions and growth strategies rather than getting mired in daily operational tasks.

However, scaling is not just about hiring more people; it's about the smart allocation of resources. It involves a careful assessment of your business's financial health and the potential return on investment from adding new team members. For instance, if a particular sector of your business is generating significant income, reinvesting a portion of that profit into expanding your team is a wise move. This reinvestment could be in hiring a specialist who can bring new expertise or increase manpower to handle increased demand.

Moreover, scaling your team should align with long-term goals and the overall vision for your business. Each new hire should not only fill an immediate need but also contribute to the broader objectives of your company. Whether it's improving customer service, expanding product lines, or entering new markets, each addition to your team should be a step toward these larger aspirations.

In summary, scaling your business requires a balanced approach. It's about growing your team in a way that aligns with your revenue growth, maintaining strategic oversight as a leader, and ensuring each new hire contributes meaningfully to your business's long-term objectives. This approach enables sustainable growth and positions your business to capitalize on opportunities while navigating challenges effectively.

Chapter 26: Getting Freelancers off the Platform & Working Directly For Your Business

Getting freelancers off the platforms and working directly for you is a transition that's a significant step and should be approached with a strategic mindset. When you initially hire freelancers through platforms like Upwork, you benefit from the security and structured processes these platforms provide. They offer a safety net in terms of payment, dispute resolution, and quality assurance. However, as your working relationship with a freelancer strengthens, and their role becomes integral to your operations, you might start considering a more direct engagement.

The financial aspect is a major factor in this decision. Platforms typically charge a fee on transactions, which can be substantial. These fees are either absorbed by the freelancer or passed on to you in part, thereby increasing the overall cost of the service. By transitioning a freelancer off-platform, you can potentially negotiate a more cost-effective arrangement. For instance, reducing the overhead costs associated with platform fees can lead to savings for you and a higher earning potential for the freelancer.

However, it's important to weigh these financial benefits against the loss of the safeguards that platforms provide. Before making the transition, consider factors such as reliability, quality of work, and consistency in meeting deadlines. A freelancer who has demonstrated a high level of professionalism and has consistently met your expectations is a more viable candidate for this transition.

Moreover, this transition is not just a financial decision but also a commitment to a deeper, more collaborative working relationship. When you bring a freelancer in-house, whether as a full-time employee or on a long-term contract, it signifies trust and a shared vision for the future. It opens opportunities for greater involvement in your business, more in-depth collaboration, and the development of a relationship that goes beyond transactional interactions.

In other words, transitioning a freelancer from a platform to a full-time role in your business can be a mutually beneficial move. It offers financial advantages and the potential for a more integrated and collaborative working relationship. However, it requires careful consideration of the freelancer's track record, the security aspects provided by the platform, and the readiness of both parties to commit to a more substantial partnership.

It's worth noting that freelancing platforms generally prefer that businesses and freelancers maintain their working relationships within the platform itself, primarily because the platform earns revenue from these interactions. If you're considering moving a freelancer off-platform for a more direct working relationship, it's important to approach this transition tactfully.

One subtle way to initiate this process is by requesting the freelancer's email address or WhatsApp contact details. Once you have their direct contact information, you can start discussing the possibility of working together outside the platform. Another approach is to arrange a voice call via Skype, Zoom, WhatsApp, or a similar service. Once the conversation moves off the platform, you have more freedom to discuss and negotiate terms directly with the freelancer.

This strategy is particularly relevant if you foresee a long-term collaboration with the freelancer or are considering transitioning them into a full-time role within your business. However, handling this process professionally is crucial, respecting the freelancers' and the platform's policies and terms of service. Transitioning off a platform should be a mutually beneficial decision, made with consideration of the potential impact on all parties involved.

Chapter 27: What Now?

As we reach the conclusion of our journey in this book, I want to leave you with a compelling call to action. You now have before you an array of tips, techniques, and strategies that can transform your small business through the power of outsourcing. The path to growth is clear, and it's time for you to take those crucial steps.

You've learned about the intricacies of selecting the right tasks to outsource, evaluating potential team members, and the vital art of delegation. We've explored the platforms that can serve as your gateway to a world of global talent and how to navigate them. You've been equipped with knowledge on managing and maintaining these relationships and, most importantly, understanding when and what not to outsource.

Now, the real work begins. It's time to put these insights into practice. Remember, knowledge is potent, but it's the application of this knowledge that brings about real change. Start small if you need to, but start nonetheless. Whether it's delegating repetitive tasks to free up your time or engaging experts for specialized roles, each step you take is a move towards scaling and growing your business.

Reflect on the areas of your business that can benefit most from outsourcing. Is it the time-consuming administrative tasks, or perhaps the need for specialized skills that your current team lacks? Maybe it's the strategic move to free up your time to focus on business development and growth. Identify these areas and begin your outsourcing journey there.

Don't let fear of the unknown hold you back. Yes, venturing into the world of outsourcing can be daunting. Yes, it requires a leap of faith to entrust aspects of your business to external partners. But the potential rewards far outweigh the risks. You're not just outsourcing tasks; you're embracing a new way of working that can bring about unparalleled growth and efficiency.

As you embark on this path, remember the importance of communication, clarity, and a shared vision with your outsourcing partners. Build relationships based on trust and mutual respect. Always keep your business's core values and goals at the forefront of your decision-making process.

In conclusion, the journey of growing your small business with outsourcing is an ongoing process. It's a dynamic and exciting path filled with opportunities for learning, innovation, and growth. The strategies and tips outlined in this book are your roadmap. Use them to navigate the outsourcing landscape, tap into global talent, and unlock the full potential of your business.

I encourage you to take the first step today. Embrace the possibilities that outsourcing offers and watch as your business transforms and reaches new heights. Remember, the only limit to your success is the extent of your willingness to embrace change and seize opportunities.